SWEET LITTLE CAKES

-FROM-
MRS. ZABAR'S BAKESHOP

For my children, grandchildren, and my husband,

who ate all the cake.

SWEET LITTLE CAKES

— FROM —

MRS. ZABAR'S
BAKESHOP

PERFECT DESSERTS FOR SHARING

TRACEY ZABAR

PHOTOGRAPHY BY ELLEN SILVERMAN

RIZZOLI
NEW YORK

New York Paris London Milan

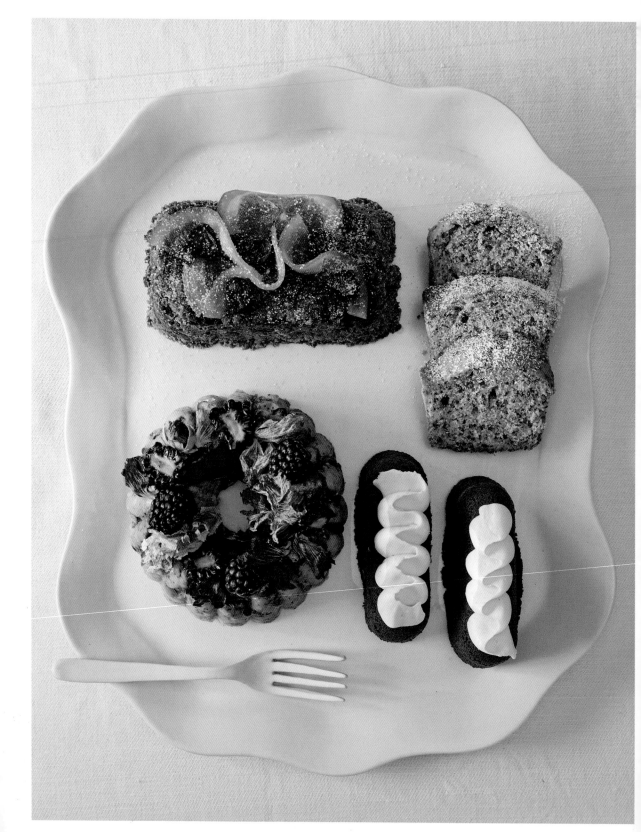

CONTENTS

INTRODUCTION

Small cakes have been enjoyed for thousands of years. Eventually honey, fruit like dates and figs, and, later, sugar were added to bread dough, which then was rolled into balls and baked, and dessert cakes and cookies evolved. Today's sweet cakes are generally made from a mixture of flour, butter, eggs, sugar, and other ingredients, and are often finished with frosting, glaze, icing, and decorations.

In my research for this baking book, I discovered some adorably named small cakes, such as kiss-me, mud pie, boy bait, little girl's cake, baby cake, fairy cake, lemon drop cake, tipsy cake, millionaire's shortbread, and polka dot cake. I also came across miniature cakes for many different occasions—for chitchats with tea, reunions, neighborhood gatherings, after-school snacks, coffee breaks and klatches, and other get-togethers, including breakup comfort visits. In my opinion, small cakes are also perfect for celebrating engagements, showers, anniversaries, and birthdays, as well as days when we welcome someone into the world and other days when we say goodbye. There are cupcakes to soothe a booboo, celebrate a milestone, or tuck into a lunchbox. What about holidays? Each one merits a cake.

Love stories often involve small cakes. At one time, a young girl reeled in the object of her affection with a courting cake, and at the end of a wedding, an even younger girl took home a slice of wedding cake wrapped in a napkin and placed it under her pillow to dream of a husband-to-be. Many of today's brides choose to have ceremonial small, tiered wedding cakes instead of showstopping towering confections. An old tradition is for the bride to include a small groom's cake, in her beloved's favorite flavor. Some delight their guests with a large selection of small cakes displayed beautifully on cake stands of varying heights and on trays decorated with miniature fruits and edible flowers. Enticing mini cupcakes are offered at a dessert bar.

Tiny, individual sweets, such as petit fours, cupcakes, pastries, and snack cakes, are charming. A small, beautifully frosted and decorated cake, perched atop a stand, can be the centerpiece and star of your dessert table. Or line a variety of them in a row. Place a knife and cake server next to each one to allow guests to take tiny slivers for a tasting plate. A sampling of these small treats is fun to create.

It used to confound me why anyone would make a small batch of baked goods. Why buy all the ingredients and do all the work to end up with two little cupcakes? But then, after years of feeding a houseful of kids and their friends, our nest became empty. Making a huge cake or pie was a mistake. After taking a little taste, it was difficult to pass up another and another. While writing and editing a number of cookbooks, I learned to take a bite and give the rest away. Then I started scaling down recipes and using smaller pans.

Miniature cakes can be made in small quantities to share with two to six or big batches for a crowd to sample. Some bakers stuff them with surprise fillings of jams or gooey chocolate. You will find many delicious cakes here to suit every sweet tooth.

While creating recipes for this book, I would spend my weekly baking time making one small cake, over and over, until I deemed it perfect. Then, on to the next. The cakes are lightened with beaten eggs, baking powder, baking soda, or yeast. The addition of fruits (fresh, dried, and zested), shredded coconut, and nuts changed each recipe in my repertoire. Chopped chocolate, chocolate chips, and perhaps a spoonful of coffee round out my list of favorite ingredients. And I am partial to whipped cream, icing, or frosting on top. Note that an unfrosted cake often looks prettier with a light dusting of sifted confectioners' sugar and a few sprinkles or some edible flowers. I am still channeling my baking obsession into perfecting the next sweet thing. Since there are thousands of flavor possibilities, it's rewarding to create a unique ingredient combination to delight your family and friends.

Still, sometimes I need to make cake for a crowd. You can, too. Just double or triple the amounts of the ingredients in your chosen recipe from this collection, and double or triple the number of pans. Or use a big pan and increase the baking time.

The featured cake recipes are for every level of baker. They are divided into the four seasons because fresh ingredients are most delicious at their peak. Of course, availability may depend on your local growing zone. Many of the cakes can be made year-round. Fresh ingredients, especially fruit, are the inspiration for a number of these cakes. Our local farmers' market often guides me when thinking about the week's dessert course and sweet treats. A favorite summer purchase is a box containing a variety of stone fruit. Many desserts that traditionally incorporate black cherries can be made instead with plums, pears, apples, or any kind of berries. In France, I was once served clafoutis with the cherry pits left in. Not for my guests—everything must be pitted. I even cut each cherry in half to check for a second pit.

I could write another dozen volumes with recipes for other types of cakes, but this baking book contains a collection of my favorites. With or without frosting, a cake is a tasty, sweet invention. Have a little cake.

NOTES ON BAKING CAKES

The little cakes in this baking book are simple to prepare. Small, manageable batches of cake are quick to whip up and perfect for two. Although I converted quantities in the recipes from metric (more precise but less familiar to most home bakers) to standard American measurements, the proportions of the ingredients have remained the same. There is a chart at the end of the book to convert measurements to metric.

Start with a clean, organized kitchen, and you can probably do the dishes and put your pantry back in order before the timer dings and your cake comes out of the oven.

Stock your kitchen with the very best appliances and tools. Although you can mix your batter by hand, a stand mixer is a great investment. My lavender one is the workhorse (besides me) of my baking kitchen. You need only one, but invest in multiple work bowls, beaters, and whisks if you plan to do a lot of baking. The same goes for measuring cups (metal and glass), measuring spoons, and silicone spatulas.

A metal offset spatula or two and a revolving cake decorating stand are optional, but useful to have on hand. Ice-cream scoops with spring-loaded handles are wonderful tools to fill the wells of cupcake and canoe pans. A nice set of round cookie cutters comes in handy, too. Don't forget a wire cooling rack and perhaps some cardboard cake rounds and boxes for transporting and sharing your cakes.

Treat yourself to good baking pans. Always avoid the nonstick and dark-colored varieties, as they absorb the heat faster and promote burned cake bottoms. Half-, quarter-, and even eighth-sheet pans are sturdier than cookie sheets, and have small, raised sides so you can bake a chocolate roll in a few minutes. Fill a shelf in your pantry with a variety of small cake pans, such as loaf, round, and heart-shaped pans. Mini Bundt pans come in many marvelous shapes, making cakelets that look like flowers, dinosaurs, and even dog biscuits.

Aluminum foil is useful to lay on the bottom of your oven to catch drips if your cake overflows a bit. A pile of parchment paper sheets, a bench scraper, and lots of small bowls should always be handy. The old method of inserting a tester into a cake after you pull it out of the oven doesn't work if the recipe has a gooey ingredient, such as chocolate chips or a chocolate filling. Invest in a digital scale to weigh chocolate and cream cheese, and an instant-read (digital) thermometer. For safety, eggs need to be cooked to 165°F for a recipe, such as meringue, that isn't going to be baked further. For fully baked treats, a temperature of at least 200°F will ensure a fully cooked batter. Be careful not to let the end of the thermometer touch the sides or bottom of a metal baking pan, as it will read the temperature of the pan, which is hotter than the cake. I use the thermometer every single time I pull something out of the oven, to check that the batter is fully cooked, then rinse the thermometer immediately. Please don't use soap, and avoid wetting the handle to protect the mechanism inside.

Piping bags (if you choose a reusable one, rinse in very hot water and never use detergent) and a variety of tips are handy, as is a cherry pitter. If your trash is many steps away, set out a large bowl or an empty, rinsed milk carton to act as your "pig." You have to dump it only once, after you finish baking.

A note on cleanliness and safety: On my first day of culinary school, we all were drilled on the rules: hair tied back and netted, short nails, no nail polish, no jewelry (except a thin, plain wedding band). No open-toed shoes, no sneakers, no clogs. And on and on and on. There were days of learning the safety handbook regarding cleanliness, safe temperatures, and good habits. I adhere to those rules now, in both professional and home settings. I wash my hands dozens of times a day and keep my kitchen perfectly clean, throw out dishes with cracks and crazing, wash towels and potholders frequently, and follow that handbook. Use the golden rule—prepare food the way you would want to have your food prepared.

The Well-Stocked Pantry

Baking staples include butter, all-purpose and cake flour, sugar, vanilla extract and paste, chocolate, baking powder, and baking soda. Always use table salt. Other more rarely used ingredients, such as unsweetened coconut and dried and fresh fruit, are easily obtainable when needed. Pure extracts, never artificial ones, are essential. I buy instant yeast in large one-pound packages and store it in the refrigerator.

Choose the best quality chocolate available. I prefer 70-percent cacao/ bittersweet chocolate, and sometimes 60-percent cacao/semisweet. Dark chocolate pistoles (also called féves or coins) and small quantities of milk and white chocolate are always in my pantry, as are lots of bittersweet dark chocolate chips. Store chocolate in a dark, cool place, but not in the refrigerator unless it is very hot in your kitchen. If you must use the fridge, seal the chocolate in a zip-top bag. You can make your own chocolate chunks by chopping pistoles by hand with a sharp knife, or in a food processor fitted with a metal blade for finely ground bits. This beats the dreaded, old-school method of hacking and sawing away at a block of chocolate. If you prefer to use chocolate chips rather than making your own chunks, choose a high-quality brand. Do not substitute chocolate chips when a recipe calls for melting baking chocolate, because the chips have substances added to keep them from melting completely. Some cooks insist on using regular cocoa powder for recipes that incorporate baking soda (as opposed to baking powder), unless they also include buttermilk, yogurt, or cream of tartar, but I prefer to use Dutch process cocoa powder. It *always* works for me.

Please use fresh, organic ingredients when possible; most everything else should also be unprocessed and chemical free. (Although I am a bit of a snob about fresh ingredients, I do occasionally make junk food exceptions for crazy add-ins, like candy and marshmallows smooshed into the mix.) Shop at the farmers' market the day of or the day before baking. Purchase seasonal fruits. Dairy products, such as heavy cream, are certainly best right from the source, if you are lucky enough to have cows as your neighbors. Unsalted butter is best for the recipes in this book. Let the butter soften for a creamy batter. Make sure your baking essentials, such as jams, spices, and dried fruit (cherries, raisins, and berries), are also fresh. Nuts, in particular, can become rancid quickly.

Large eggs are ideal—again, as fresh as possible. Crack each egg individually into a small, white ceramic bowl, and take a moment to look for bits of shells,

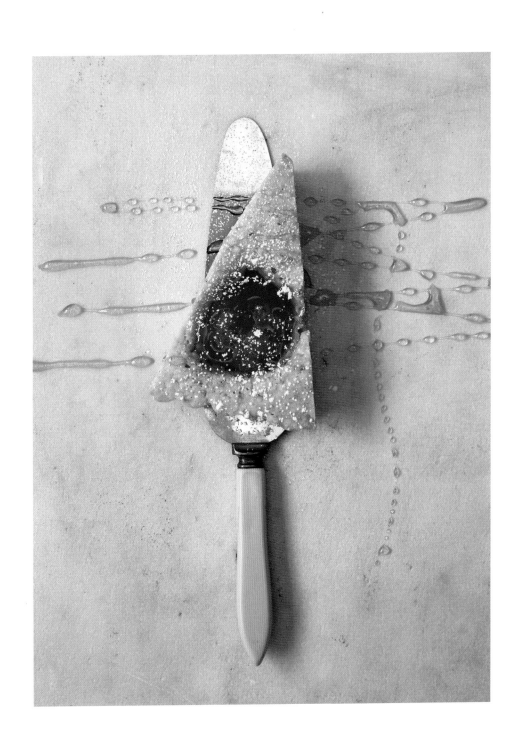

which you will need to fish out. Discard an egg if there are any blood spots and then start again with a clean bowl. Add one egg at a time to the batter, and then crack and check the next one. Stay safe—no tasting the batter, as consuming raw eggs can be dangerous to your health.

Recipe Instructions

Before you bake, study the recipe. Sometimes the instructions require placing the finished cake in the refrigerator to set, or letting a yeast batter rise, so plan ahead timewise. Take this information into consideration if you intend to whip up a cake quickly. Follow instructions carefully. Preheat the oven and butter or line your pan with parchment paper, as directed.

Note that each recipe for an icing, frosting, glaze, or other finishing topping yields enough for one cake.

A Few Basic Techniques

A practice I highly recommend is to prepare your baking setup by putting every-thing in place (this is known as *mise en place*), measuring out each ingredient and laying out each piece of equipment needed. You will be able to tell right away if there is enough (or none) of a particular ingredient, or if it isn't fresh. Go to the store to fill in missing items before baking. The beauty of preparing your *mise en place* is that if you are interrupted during baking, you'll be able to continue without missing a beat. Upon returning to the kitchen from answering the door or phone (or anything else that calls you away), you'll know where you left off. Otherwise, you run the risk of adding twice as much of an ingredient, such as sugar, which most kids would say is a forgivable sin, or, heaven forbid, not adding any sugar at all. Flour (always spooned into a measuring cup, never scooped and packed) and other dry ingredients can be dumped into a bowl or onto a sheet of parchment paper and set aside until needed. Flour comes pre-sifted, but you may have to sift confectioners' sugar, if it has lumps.

Master the basics of baking, and then experiment. Although you have to measure ingredients exactly, after you successfully bake a cake a few times, there are areas you can change a bit. For a richer flavor, try substituting vanilla bean paste or the seeds scraped from a vanilla bean for pure vanilla extract, or an envelope of vanilla-scented Italian leavening for baking soda or baking powder. You can always change the flavor of a cake by replacing an ingredient, such as raspberry jam with cherry preserves, or even everyone's childhood favorite, grape jelly.

To prevent sticking, cool a cake in a Bundt pan for 10 minutes, then remove the cake from the pan and cool completely on a wire rack. Other cakes should come out of the pans easily if the pans are lined with parchment paper and/or buttered well.

Here's how you can become a master cook and baker: Once a week, make one new savory dish and one new dessert. Keep the recipes you love in a file, on paper, or on your computer. At the end of the year, even if only half the recipes are amazing, you will have quite a repertoire.

Enjoy baking like a skilled professional, and share your new favorite cakes with a friend or two. Make an extra cake for someone who is lonely or home-bound, or for new parents. A thoughtful gift like this, especially if you include a beautiful pan or a pretty plate (and a copy of the recipe, too), will bring great joy. Go into the kitchen and start baking.

CHAPTER

№ *1*

FALL

BANANA CAKE

This cake is my son Danny's favorite treat. It is moist and filled with chocolate chips. For a special occasion, dress it up with a sweet cream cheese frosting, or leave it plain for an everyday snack. Either way, it's a lovely dessert. · MAKES ONE 6-INCH LOAF CAKE (SERVES 4)

3 tablespoons unsalted butter, softened, plus more for the pan

2 tablespoons granulated sugar, plus more for the pan

2 tablespoons packed light brown sugar

1 large egg

½ teaspoon pure vanilla extract

1 tablespoon full-fat sour cream

1 banana, roughly mashed

1 cup all-purpose flour

½ teaspoon baking soda

Pinch of salt

2 tablespoons chocolate chips

Cream Cheese Frosting, recipe follows

Preheat the oven to 350°F. Butter a 6-inch baby loaf pan. Sprinkle some granulated sugar into the pan, shake to coat, discard the excess, and set aside.

In the bowl of a stand mixer fitted with the paddle attachment, mix the remaining 3 tablespoons butter, the remaining 2 tablespoons granulated sugar, and the brown sugar. With the mixer running, add the egg, vanilla, and sour cream, then the banana and beat until the ingredients are incorporated but there are still lumps of banana remaining. Add the flour, baking soda, and salt and mix just until combined. With a silicone spatula, fold in the chocolate chips.

Scrape into the prepared pan and bake until golden brown and set, about 45 minutes. Cool completely in the pan before removing the cake from the pan. Pipe or spread the frosting on top of the cake.

recipe continues

CREAM CHEESE FROSTING

3 ounces full-fat block cream cheese, softened

1½ tablespoons unsalted butter, softened

¼ teaspoon pure vanilla extract

¾ cup confectioners' sugar

In the bowl of a stand mixer fitted with the whisk attachment, whip the cream cheese, butter, and vanilla. Add the confectioners' sugar and beat until smooth.

HONEY CAKE

This is one of my favorite cakes to bake in the fall. The spices perfume the house and I feel it is time to sharpen my pencils and head back to school. I use hazelnut coffee and orange blossom honey for this sticky, sweet dessert. Sometimes I even throw in a few tablespoons of chocolate chips. After baking and cooling, this cake caves in the center: it's best to flip it over so the glaze can be poured onto a nice, flat surface. • MAKES ONE 6-INCH LOAF CAKE (SERVES 4)

2 tablespoons unsalted butter, softened, plus more for the pan

2 teaspoons granulated sugar, plus more for the pan

¼ cup runny honey

3 tablespoons strong black coffee

¾ cup all-purpose flour

½ teaspoon baking powder

¼ teaspoon baking soda

¼ teaspoon ground cinnamon

⅛ teaspoon ground cloves

⅛ teaspoon ground nutmeg

⅛ teaspoon ground ginger

Pinch of salt

2 tablespoons packed light brown sugar

1 large egg yolk

Orange Glaze, recipe follows

Pieces of honeycomb, for finishing

Preheat the oven to 350°F. Butter a 6-inch baby loaf pan. Sprinkle some granulated sugar into the pan, shake to coat, discard the excess, and set aside.

In a small saucepan, boil the honey and coffee, then let cool for 15 minutes.

In a medium bowl, whisk together the flour, baking powder, baking soda, cinnamon, cloves, nutmeg, ginger, and salt and set aside.

In the bowl of a stand mixer fitted with the paddle attachment, cream the remaining 2 tablespoons butter, the remaining 2 teaspoons granulated sugar, and the brown sugar. Add the egg yolk and beat to combine. Add one-third of the honey-coffee mixture and beat to incorporate, then add one-third of the dry

recipe continues

ingredients, again beating to incorporate. Repeat in two more additions, and mix just until combined after you have added the remaining dry ingredients.

Scrape into the prepared pan, smooth the top, and bake until set, about 40 minutes. Cool completely in the pan. Remove the cake from the pan, flip it over, and drizzle the glaze on the flat side. Top with honeycomb.

ORANGE GLAZE

½ cup confectioners' sugar, sifted

2 to 3 teaspoons freshly squeezed orange juice

In a small bowl, mix the confectioners' sugar with enough juice to make a thin glaze with no lumps.

PECAN BARS

Is this a cake? Or a pie? Or some form of cookie? Is it a cousin of the brookie (part brownie, part cookie)? It doesn't matter because these yummy squares are sweet and gooey. They are a favorite of my pecan pie–loving son Michael.

• MAKES TEN 1½ BY 4-INCH BARS OR FOUR 4-INCH SQUARES (SERVES 4 TO 5)

CRUST

⅓ cup granulated sugar

8 tablespoons unsalted butter, softened

1 tablespoon heavy cream

1 cup all-purpose flour

FILLING

2 large eggs

⅓ cup light corn syrup

½ cup packed light brown sugar

3 tablespoons unsalted butter, melted

1 tablespoon pure vanilla bean paste

1 tablespoon heavy cream

Pinch of salt

1½ cups pecan halves

½ cup chocolate chips

Preheat the oven to 350°F. Line an 8-inch square pan with parchment paper, and set aside.

To make the crust, in the bowl of a stand mixer fitted with the paddle attachment, cream the granulated sugar and butter. Add the cream, then the flour, mix just until combined, and press into the prepared pan. (Leave the paddle attachment on the mixer, and return the unwashed bowl to the mixer.)

Bake the crust until it starts to brown on the edges, about 20 minutes. Let the crust cool a bit while you prepare the filling, leaving the oven on.

To make the filling, add the eggs to the bowl of the mixer and beat them, then add the corn syrup, brown sugar, melted butter, vanilla bean paste, cream, and salt and mix until well combined.

Pour the filling onto the crust, and scatter a layer of pecans over the top, then scatter the chocolate chips on top of the nuts. Bake about 30 minutes.

Cool completely in the pan, then refrigerate in the pan for at least 1 hour. Remove the cake from the pan, discard the parchment paper, trim the edges, and cut into 1½ by 4-inch bars or 4-inch squares.

APPLE CAKE

This is an updated old-lady recipe, made by many a grandma. It is a perfect dessert for fall when apples are at their prime. Long ago, a relative served a similar cake, and I begged for the recipe. She never shared it, and I later found out the cake came from her local bakery—not her kitchen. • MAKES ONE 5-INCH BUNDT CAKE (SERVES 4)

3 tablespoons unsalted butter, softened, plus more for the pan	Pinch of salt
	1 large egg
½ small apple, peeled, cored, and cut into ½-inch cubes	1 teaspoon pure vanilla extract
	¾ cup all-purpose flour
⅔ cup plus ½ teaspoon granulated sugar, divided	1 teaspoon baking powder
	¼ cup pecan or walnut halves
1 teaspoon packed light brown sugar	Confectioners' sugar, for dusting
¼ teaspoon ground cinnamon	Dried apple slices, for topping

Preheat the oven to 350°F. Butter one 5-inch well of a Bundt quartet pan, and set aside.

In a medium bowl, toss the apple cubes with the ½ teaspoon granulated sugar, the brown sugar, and cinnamon and set aside.

In the bowl of a stand mixer fitted with the paddle attachment, cream the remaining 3 tablespoons of butter, the remaining ⅔ cup granulated sugar, and salt. Add the egg and vanilla and beat to incorporate. Add the flour and baking powder, and mix just until combined. With a silicone spatula, fold in the nuts, and then scrape half the batter into the prepared pan.

Add the apple-sugar mixture on top of the batter, being careful not to let the mixture touch the center tube or edges. Add the remaining batter, and gently smooth the top with a silicone spatula.

Bake until browned and set, about 30 minutes. Cool for 10 minutes in the pan, then remove the cake from the hot pan and cool it completely on a wire rack. Dust with confectioners' sugar, and top with dried apple slices.

ALMOND-TOPPED CAKE

In England, I tasted a few varieties of this type of dessert, often called plum cake or plum pudding, with fruit (traditionally raisins or currants) added but, interestingly, no plums. This rustic cake is made with confectioners' sugar, resulting in a tender and light crumb. It is wonderful served with caramel sauce on the side. You can substitute other types of dried fruit or candied or fresh fruit for the raisins. I make it with blueberries; pitted and halved cherries; diced peeled pear; apple chunks; or sometimes, even plums.

• MAKES ONE 6-INCH LOAF CAKE (SERVES 4)

4 tablespoons unsalted butter, softened, plus more for the pan

Granulated sugar, for the pan

½ cup confectioners' sugar

1 large egg

1 large egg yolk

½ teaspoon pure vanilla extract

1 cup cake flour

¾ teaspoon baking powder

¼ teaspoon salt

½ cup raisins

3 tablespoons sliced almonds

Preheat the oven to 350°F. Butter a 6-inch baby loaf pan. Sprinkle some granulated sugar into the pan, shake to coat, discard the excess, and set aside.

In the bowl of a stand mixer fitted with the paddle attachment, cream the remaining 4 tablespoons butter and the confectioners' sugar. Add the egg, egg yolk, and vanilla and mix until incorporated. Add the flour, baking powder, and salt and mix just until combined.

With a silicone spatula, fold in the raisins. Scrape the batter into the prepared pan, sprinkle or layer the almonds on top, and press the almonds down gently so they stick to the batter.

Bake until set, about 45 minutes. Cool completely in the pan before removing the cake from the pan.

DATE CAKE

My friend Nick Malgieri and I have been searching for a recipe for a date-nut loaf cake that was sold in supermarkets in the 1960s. Sticky and dark, its sweetness was tempered with a good slathering of cream cheese on each slice. We never found that recipe, but here is a very different one, similar to a typical ladies' magazine recipe from long ago, which is pretty wonderful, too.

• MAKES ONE 6-INCH LOAF CAKE (SERVES 4)

1 tablespoon unsalted butter,
   softened, plus more for the pan
½ cup pitted, halved dates
½ cup boiling water
¼ cup packed light brown sugar
1 large egg yolk

Finely grated zest of ½ orange
¾ cup all-purpose flour
¾ teaspoon baking soda
¼ teaspoon salt
Confectioners' sugar, for dusting

Preheat the oven to 350°F. Butter a 6-inch baby loaf pan, and set aside.

Place the dates in a heatproof bowl. Pour the boiling water over them. Allow to cool until slightly warm, and set aside.

In the bowl of a stand mixer fitted with the paddle attachment, cream the remaining 1 tablespoon butter with the brown sugar. Add the egg yolk and beat to incorporate, then beat in the orange zest. Add the dates and their soaking water. When the dates are incorporated (the batter will be lumpy), add the flour, baking soda, and salt and mix just until combined.

Scrape into the prepared pan. Bake until set, about 30 minutes. Cool completely in the pan before removing the cake from the pan and dust confectioners' sugar on top.

SNACK CAKES

Here's my oft-requested recipe for whoopie pies, baked in the shape of another famous snack, Twinkies. I have been making these Massachusetts treats since I was little. It's impossible to bake a smaller quantity as you would have to split the egg yolk into halves or quarters. Trust me, they're so good that even a batch of eight won't last long. · MAKES EIGHT 4-INCH "CANOE" CAKES (SERVES 8)

4 tablespoons unsalted butter, softened, plus more for the pan

½ cup granulated sugar

1 large egg yolk

½ cup whole milk

1 teaspoon pure vanilla extract

¼ cup Dutch process cocoa powder

¾ teaspoon baking soda

¼ teaspoon baking powder

Pinch of salt

1 cup all-purpose flour

Marshmallow Filling, recipe follows

Preheat the oven to 350°F. Lightly butter eight 4-inch wells of a "canoe" pan, and set aside.

In the bowl of a stand mixer fitted with the paddle attachment, cream the remaining 4 tablespoons butter and the granulated sugar. Add the egg yolk, milk, and vanilla. Add the cocoa powder, baking soda, baking powder, and salt. Add the flour and mix just until combined.

Using a silicone spatula and a soupspoon, divide the batter evenly among the wells of the prepared pan and smooth the tops with the spatula.

Bake until set, 12 to 15 minutes. Cool in the pan for 10 minutes, then remove the cakes from the hot pan and cool completely on a wire rack.

When the cakes are completely cool, scrape the filling into a pastry bag fitted with a small plain tip. On the bottom of each cake, push the tip ¼ inch into a spot a third of the way from the small end and pipe a small amount of filling into the cake. Repeat, using a spot the same distance from the other small end of the cake. Be careful not to push the tip in too much, as you will pierce

recipe continues

the cake and the filling will squirt out of the top! It will still be yummy, but messy. Pipe the remaining filling on top of the cakes using the small plain tip or a decorative one.

MARSHMALLOW FILLING

8 tablespoons unsalted butter,
   softened
½ cup Marshmallow Fluff

½ teaspoon pure vanilla extract
½ cup confectioners' sugar
Whole milk, as needed

In the bowl of a stand mixer fitted with the whisk attachment, whip the butter, Marshmallow Fluff, and vanilla. Add the confectioner' sugar and beat until smooth. Thin with a little milk, if needed, to make it easy to pipe.

TEA-FLAVORED COFFEE-BREAK CAKE

I often put some coffee in my cake batters, especially those containing chocolate. With this cake, for the first time I dumped in tea leaves—the result is yummy. Use your favorite flavor of tea (I use English breakfast, orange pekoe, or green tea) and runny honey. · MAKES ONE 6-INCH LOAF CAKE (SERVES 4)

2 tablespoons unsalted butter, softened, plus more for the pan

3 tablespoons granulated sugar

2 tea bags

1 large egg

2 tablespoons heavy cream

1 teaspoon honey, preferably orange blossom

½ teaspoon pure vanilla extract

½ cup all-purpose flour

½ teaspoon baking powder

Pinch of salt

Confectioners' sugar, for dusting

Candied lemon peel, for serving

Whipped Cream with Orange Zest, for serving, recipe follows

Preheat the oven to 350°F. Butter a 6-inch baby loaf pan, and set aside.

In the bowl of a stand mixer fitted with the paddle attachment, cream the remaining 2 tablespoons butter and the granulated sugar. Tear open the tea bags and dump the contents into the batter. Discard the tea bags. Mix the batter to combine. Add the egg and beat to incorporate, then add the cream, honey, and vanilla and beat to incorporate. Add the flour, baking powder, and salt and mix just until combined.

Scrape the batter into the prepared pan. Bake until set, about 30 minutes. Cool the cake in the pan completely on a wire rack. Remove the cake from the pan and dust with confectioners' sugar. Serve with candied lemon peel and whipped cream.

recipe continues

WHIPPED CREAM WITH ORANGE ZEST

1 cup heavy cream

1 tablespoon granulated sugar

½ teaspoon pure vanilla extract

⅛ teaspoon cream of tartar

Finely grated zest of ½ orange

Pinch of salt

In the bowl of a stand mixer fitted with the whisk attachment, start whipping the cream and as it thickens, gradually add the granulated sugar. Add the vanilla, cream of tartar, orange zest, and salt and whip until stiff peaks form.

CRANBERRY-ORANGE CAKE

This festive little loaf is perfect for Thanksgiving (thanks to my friends Janet and Ellie for sharing their favorite holiday dessert) or simply snack time. You can replace the fruit and nuts called for in the recipe with a mixture of alternatives, such as berries and pistachios. • MAKES ONE 6-INCH LOAF CAKE (SERVES 4)

1 tablespoon unsalted butter, softened, plus more for the pan

¼ cup granulated sugar, plus more for the pan and finishing

2 tablespoons packed light brown sugar

1 large egg yolk

1 tablespoon finely grated orange zest

1 teaspoon full-fat sour cream

½ teaspoon pure vanilla extract

¼ cup freshly squeezed orange juice

½ cup all-purpose flour

½ teaspoon baking powder

¼ teaspoon baking soda

¼ teaspoon salt

½ cup raisins

½ cup fresh (or plumped dried) cranberries

⅓ cup pecans, roughly chopped

Dried cranberries, for finishing

Candied orange slices, for finishing

Preheat the oven to 350°F. Butter a 6-inch baby loaf pan. Sprinkle some granulated sugar into the pan, shake to coat, discard the excess, and set aside.

In the bowl of a stand mixer fitted with the paddle attachment, cream the remaining 1 tablespoon butter, ¼ cup granulated sugar, and the brown sugar. Add the egg yolk, orange zest, sour cream, and vanilla and beat to incorporate. Add the orange juice and flour in two additions each, beating to incorporate between the additions, then add the baking powder, baking soda, and salt and mix just until combined. With a silicone spatula, fold in the raisins, fresh cranberries, and pecans.

Scrape into the prepared pan and bake until set, about 40 minutes. Cool completely in the pan before removing the cake from the pan. Plump the dried cranberries for finishing in hot water for 15 minutes, drain, and sprinkle them and the candied orange slices on top. Finish by sprinkling granulated sugar on top.

PUMPKIN CAKE

Here's a little treat for your fall baking repertoire. The next time you make a pumpkin pie, steal a small bit of the puree for this recipe. Or make more cakes as gifts for your friends by using the whole can of puree. • MAKES ONE 6-INCH LOAF CAKE (SERVES 4)

2 tablespoons unsalted butter,
    plus more for the pan
¼ cup granulated sugar
1 tablespoon packed light
    brown sugar
¼ cup pumpkin puree
    (not pie filling)
1 large egg yolk
½ teaspoon baking powder
¼ teaspoon baking soda

¼ teaspoon ground cinnamon
⅛ teaspoon ground cloves
⅛ teaspoon ground ginger
⅛ teaspoon ground nutmeg
Pinch of salt
½ cup all-purpose flour
½ cup chocolate chips
¼ cup pecan or walnut halves,
    plus more for topping

Preheat the oven to 350°F. Butter a 6-inch baby loaf pan, and set aside.

In the bowl of a stand mixer fitted with the paddle attachment, cream the remaining 2 tablespoons butter, and the granulated and brown sugars. Add the pumpkin puree and egg yolk and beat to incorporate. Add the baking powder, baking soda, cinnamon, cloves, ginger, nutmeg, and salt and mix until incorporated. Add the flour and mix just until combined.

With a silicone spatula, fold in the chocolate chips and ¼ cup of the nuts. Transfer to the prepared pan and top with more nuts.

Bake until set, about 45 minutes. Cool completely in the pan before removing the cake from the pan.

PEAR CAKE

I once spent weeks baking all types of cakes from my grandparents' native Sicily and Austria. This is a combination of two of my favorite recipes, one from each town in the "old country." I sometimes add a bit of orange extract to this little cake, and finish with a bunch of champagne grapes or fresh currants. Enjoy this flavorful torta/kuchen. • MAKES ONE 5-INCH BUNDT CAKE (SERVES 4)

4 tablespoons unsalted butter, softened, plus more for the pan

½ cup granulated sugar

1 large egg

½ teaspoon pure vanilla bean paste

¼ teaspoon pure orange extract (optional)

¾ cup all-purpose flour

½ teaspoon baking powder

¼ teaspoon baking soda

¼ teaspoon ground cinnamon

Pinch of salt

½ ripe pear, peeled, cored, and cubed

2 tablespoons packed light brown sugar

Pear slices, for finishing

Confectioners' sugar, for dusting

Preheat the oven to 350°F. Butter one well of a 5-inch Bundt quartet pan, and set aside.

In the bowl of a stand mixer fitted with the paddle attachment, cream the remaining 4 tablespoons butter and the granulated sugar. Add the egg, vanilla bean paste, and orange extract (if using) and beat to incorporate. Add the flour, baking powder, baking soda, cinnamon, and salt and mix just until combined.

Scrape half the batter into the prepared pan, then sprinkle on the pear cubes first, followed by the brown sugar, being careful not to let either touch the center tube or edges. Add the remaining batter, and gently smooth the top with a silicone spatula.

Bake until browned and set, about 30 minutes. Cool for 10 minutes in the pan, then remove the cake from the hot pan and cool completely on a wire rack. Finish with pear slices. Dust with confectioners' sugar.

JAM CAKE

This type of spice cake is traditionally made with blackberry preserves, but you can use any flavor jam you like. People often add allspice, ginger, or raisins, and sometimes, even applesauce. · MAKES ONE 4-INCH ROUND CAKE (SERVES 4)

4 tablespoons unsalted butter, softened, plus more for the pans

½ cup granulated sugar

¼ cup packed light brown sugar

1 large egg

1 large egg yolk

½ cup fruit jam or preserves or marmalade

¼ cup heavy cream

1 tablespoon full-fat sour cream

1 teaspoon molasses

¼ teaspoon pure vanilla extract

½ teaspoon ground cinnamon

¼ teaspoon ground cloves

¼ teaspoon ground nutmeg

1¼ cups all-purpose flour

1 teaspoon baking powder

¼ teaspoon salt

¼ cup pecan or walnut halves, coarsely chopped

Vanilla Bean Frosting, recipe follows

Edible flowers, for decorating

Preheat the oven to 350°F. Butter the sides of two 4-inch round pans with 2-inch sides. Place a round of parchment paper in the bottom of each pan, and set aside.

In the bowl of a stand mixer fitted with the paddle attachment, cream the remaining 4 tablespoons butter with the granulated and brown sugars. Add the egg and egg yolk and beat to incorporate, then add the jam, heavy cream, sour cream, molasses, and vanilla and mix to incorporate. Add the cinnamon, cloves, and nutmeg and mix to incorporate. Finally, add the flour, baking powder, and salt and mix just until combined. With a silicone spatula, fold in the nuts.

Scrape into the prepared pans and bake until set, about 25 minutes. Cool for 10 minutes in the pans, then remove the cakes from the hot pans. Cool completely on a wire rack.

recipe continues

Using a serrated knife, trim off the dome of each cake and discard (or eat). Place one layer on a platter, bottom (flat) side up, and peel off the parchment round. Spread one-third of the frosting on top. Place the second layer of cake on top, bottom (flat) side up, and peel off the parchment round. Spread the remaining frosting on the top and sides of the cake, and decorate with edible flowers.

VANILLA BEAN FROSTING

12 tablespoons unsalted butter, softened

½ teaspoon pure vanilla bean paste

3 cups confectioners' sugar

Pinch of salt

2 teaspoons pure maple syrup (optional)

1 to 2 tablespoons heavy cream, if needed

In the bowl of a stand mixer fitted with the whisk attachment, whip the butter and vanilla bean paste. Add the confectioners' sugar and salt. Add the maple syrup (if using). Whip until thickened. Add a small amount of cream, if needed, to reach a spreadable consistency.

CHAPTER

№ 2

WINTER

CITRUS POPPY SEED CAKE

Poppy seed cake is often made with too much lemon and a sticky, overly sweet glaze. Try my take on this old favorite. If desired, substitute lemon, lime, clementine, or tangerine zest and juice for the orange. Serve with candied orange peel on the side. • MAKES ONE 5-INCH BUNDT CAKE (SERVES 4)

2 tablespoons unsalted butter,
    plus more for the pan
½ cup granulated sugar
Finely grated zest of ¼ orange
1 large egg
¼ cup heavy cream
1 teaspoon freshly squeezed
    orange juice

½ teaspoon pure vanilla extract
2 tablespoons poppy seeds
½ cup all-purpose flour
½ teaspoon baking powder
Pinch of salt
Confectioners' sugar, for dusting

Preheat the oven to 350°F. Butter one 5-inch well of a Bundt quartet pan, and set aside.

In the bowl of a stand mixer fitted with the paddle attachment, cream the remaining 2 tablespoons butter and the granulated sugar. Add the orange zest and egg and beat until combined, then add the cream, orange juice, and vanilla and beat to combine. Add the poppy seeds and mix until incorporated. Add the flour, baking powder, and salt and mix just until combined.

Scrape into the prepared pan and bake until the edges start to brown and the cake is set, about 35 minutes. Cool for 10 minutes in the pan, then remove the cake from the hot pan and allow to cool completely on a wire rack. Dust with confectioners' sugar before serving.

BABKA
with choice of four fillings

This babka recipe is from a long-lost cousin who worked in a bakery many years ago. The fillings have varied over the years, per my family's requests. You can make all four babkas with the same filling, or mix them up. For example, if baking four chocolate babkas, make a quadruple batch of the Chocolate Filling and Drizzle. Other filling variations to consider are poppy seed, cheese, apple, or raisin. I like to use berries and figs when they are in season. Many old-school bakeries either bake a streusel on each babka or, once cooled, add a thick layer of confectioners' sugar on top and then drizzle melted chocolate on top of the sugar. I prefer to skip the streusel and sugar topping, and just use the drizzle. However you top it, babka is a *bubbe*-worthy treat, especially when you slice it and make it into decadent French toast, with crème anglaise or chocolate sauce on the side. • MAKES DOUGH FOR FOUR 6-INCH BABKAS (EACH SERVES 4)

¾ cup whole milk or heavy cream, heated to 90°F

1 tablespoon instant yeast

3 tablespoons plus 2 teaspoons granulated sugar, plus more for the pans

3 tablespoons unsalted butter, softened, plus more for the bowl and pans

3 large eggs, at room temperature

2 teaspoons pure vanilla bean paste

3¾ cups all-purpose flour, plus more for rolling

½ teaspoon salt

In a small bowl, mix the milk or heavy cream, yeast, and 2 teaspoons granulated sugar. Let sit until foamy, about 10 minutes.

In the bowl of a stand mixer fitted with the paddle attachment, cream the 3 tablespoons butter and 3 tablespoons granulated sugar. Add the eggs and beat to incorporate, then add the milk-yeast mixture and vanilla bean paste, and mix. Add the 3¾ cups flour and salt and mix just until combined.

recipe continues

Butter a large bowl. Place the dough in the buttered bowl, cover with plastic wrap, and let it sit in a warm, draft-free place until doubled in volume, for about 1 hour.

CHOCOLATE BABKA

CHOCOLATE BABKA FILLING AND DRIZZLE
makes enough for one 6-inch babka

3 tablespoons unsalted butter

3 ounces bittersweet or
  semisweet chocolate,
  coarsely chopped

3 tablespoons granulated sugar

1½ teaspoons Dutch process
  cocoa powder

Pinch of salt

3 tablespoons chocolate chips,
  for sprinkling on the filling

In the top of a double boiler, melt the butter and chopped chocolate. Remove the top of the double boiler from the heat, stir, and add the granulated sugar, cocoa, and salt. Leave the bottom of the double boiler, partially filled with water, on the stove for finishing the babkas. Let the filling cool for 15 minutes.

STREUSEL (OPTIONAL)
makes enough for one 6-inch babka

¼ cup all-purpose flour

2 tablespoons packed light
  brown sugar

1 teaspoon ground cinnamon

Pinch of salt

4 tablespoons cold unsalted butter,
  cut into ½-inch cubes

In a medium bowl, toss together the flour, brown sugar, cinnamon, and salt. Add the butter and mix, leaving small lumps of butter that are not incorporated. Set aside.

Butter four 6-inch baby loaf pans. Sprinkle some granulated sugar into each pan, shake to coat, and discard the excess. Line a half-sheet pan with parchment paper and set aside.

Place a new piece of parchment paper on the counter and sprinkle it with a small amount of flour. Cut the dough into 4 equal pieces. Place one piece of the dough on the floured parchment paper and sprinkle a bit more flour on top of it. Place another piece of parchment paper on top of the dough and, using a rolling pin on top of the parchment, roll it out until it is a ⅛-inch-thick rough rectangle. Remove the top piece of parchment.

If making the chocolate babka, scrape about three-quarters of the filling on top. Place the remaining filling in the top of the double boiler. (For the other fillings, follow the steps outlined for each on pages 56 and 57.) Spread the filling on the dough with a metal offset spatula, leaving a 1-inch border all around. Sprinkle the chocolate chips on top of the filling.

Roll up the dough like a jelly roll and tuck in both sides. Gently press the dough so that all edges are sealed, then twist the dough, fold it in half, and place in the prepared pan. If using the streusel, with the side of your hand, make a lengthwise dent in the top of the babka, and sprinkle the streusel on top.

Repeat with the other three babkas. Set them in a warm, draft-free place until they rise, for about 30 minutes. Meanwhile, preheat the oven to 350°F.

Bake the babkas for about 40 minutes. The tops will puff up quite high. Cool completely in the pans. If making chocolate babkas, melt the reserved filling in the top of the double boiler and drizzle on top of the cooled babkas, then remove the babkas from the pans.

recipe continues

VARIATION:

PEANUT BUTTER AND JELLY BABKA FILLING

makes enough for one 6-inch babka

¼ cup creamy peanut butter

⅓ cup jam or preserves, preferably
   apricot or peach

3 tablespoons packed light brown
   sugar, for sprinkling

After rolling out the dough, spread the peanut butter on top, leaving a 1-inch border all the way around. Spread the jam or preserves on top of the peanut butter, then roll up the dough like a jelly roll and tuck in both sides. Gently press the dough so that all edges are sealed, then twist the dough, fold it in half, and place in the prepared loaf pan.

Sprinkle the brown sugar on top. Set it in a warm, draft-free place until it rises, for about 30 minutes. Meanwhile, preheat the oven to 350°F.

Bake the babka until set, about 40 minutes. The top will puff up quite high. Cool completely in the pan before removing the cake from the pan.

VARIATION:

HAZELNUT–CHOCOLATE CHIP BABKA FILLING

makes enough for one 6-inch babka

¼ cup store-bought hazelnut spread

¼ cup chocolate chips

2 tablespoons packed light brown
   sugar, for sprinkling

After rolling out the dough, spread the hazelnut spread on top, leaving a 1-inch border all the way around. Sprinkle the chocolate chips on top, then roll up the dough like a jelly roll and tuck in both sides. Gently press the dough so that all edges are sealed, then twist the dough, fold it in half, and place in the prepared loaf pan.

Sprinkle the brown sugar on top. Set it in a warm, draft-free place until it rises, for about 30 minutes. Meanwhile, preheat the oven to 350°F.

Bake the babka until set, about 40 minutes. The top will puff up quite high. Cool completely in the pan before removing the cake from the pan.

BERRY OR FIG BABKA FILLING

makes enough for one 6-inch babka

¼ cup berry or fig preserves

½ cup fresh raspberries

2 tablespoons granulated sugar, for sprinkling

After rolling out the dough, spread the berry or fig preserves on top, leaving a ¾-inch border all the way around. Sprinkle fresh raspberries on top, then roll up the dough like a jelly roll and tuck in both sides. Gently press the dough so that all edges are sealed, then twist the dough, fold it in half, and place in the prepared loaf pan.

Sprinkle the granulated sugar on top. Set it in a warm, draft-free place until it rises, for about 30 minutes. Meanwhile, preheat the oven to 350°F.

Bake the babka until set, about 40 minutes. The top will puff up quite high. Cool completely in the pan before removing the cake from the pan.

CHOCOLATE CAKE
with choice of four fillings

I get a little nervous when I cut open a lovely cake and there is molten chocolate flowing out. Is it uncooked batter, or a tunnel of fudge? However, I do love something yummy and surprising in the middle. Start with this recipe for the rich chocolate cake base. The varied fillings change the character of the cake. Thanks, and a tip of the hat, to baker extraordinaire Jenny Kellerhals, who made my coconut-filled version even more yummy. • MAKES ONE 5-INCH BUNDT CAKE (SERVES 4)

CHOCOLATE BATTER

5 tablespoons unsalted butter,
   plus more for the pan
1½ ounces bittersweet or semisweet
   chocolate, chopped
2 tablespoons plus 1½ teaspoons
   Dutch process cocoa powder
⅓ cup granulated sugar
1 large egg

¼ cup full-fat sour cream
½ teaspoon pure vanilla extract
½ cup cake flour
½ teaspoon baking powder
Pinch of salt
Filling of your choice, see following
   pages

Preheat the oven to 350°F. Butter one 5-inch well of a quartet Bundt pan, and set aside.

In the top of a double boiler, melt the remaining 5 tablespoons butter and the bittersweet chocolate. Remove the top from the heat and cool for 10 minutes. Add the cocoa powder, stir to incorporate and set aside.

In the bowl of a stand mixer fitted with the paddle attachment, beat the granulated sugar and egg. Slowly add the butter-chocolate mixture and mix to incorporate. Beat in the sour cream and vanilla. Add the flour, baking powder, and salt and mix just until combined.

recipe continues

Add half the chocolate batter to the prepared pan. Dollop and smooth the filling you are using on top, being careful not to let the filling touch the center tube or edges. Add the remaining batter, and gently smooth the top with a silicone spatula.

Bake until set, about 25 minutes. Cool for 10 minutes in the pan, then remove the cake from the hot pan and cool completely on a wire rack.

COCONUT FILLING AND TOPPING

1 large egg white
1 tablespoon granulated sugar
⅓ cup unsweetened shredded
   coconut

2 tablespoons store-bought
   chocolate syrup, for drizzling
Toasted coconut flakes,
   for finishing

In a medium bowl, use a fork to beat the egg white until it is frothy and starts to become opaque. Whisk in the granulated sugar, then mix in the coconut. Use this mixture as the filling.

To finish, drizzle the chocolate syrup on top of the cooled cake, and sprinkle toasted coconut flakes onto the syrup.

PEANUT BUTTER FILLING AND TOPPING

2 tablespoons peanut butter,
   creamy or chunky
   (but not natural)

1 tablespoon confectioners'
   sugar, plus more for dusting

In the clean bowl of a stand mixer fitted with the whisk attachment, beat the peanut butter and 1 tablespoon confectioners' sugar until smooth. Use this mixture as the filling.

Dust the cooled cake with additional confectioners' sugar.

CHOCOLATE CHIP–CREAM CHEESE FILLING

2 ounces full-fat block cream cheese,
    softened
1 large egg white

1 tablespoon granulated sugar
¼ teaspoon pure vanilla extract
1 tablespoon chocolate chips

In the bowl of a stand mixer fitted with the whisk attachment, whip the cream cheese, egg white, granulated sugar, and vanilla. With a silicone spatula, fold in the chocolate chips. Use this mixture as the filling.

JAM FILLING

¼ cup jam or marmalade

Use this as the filling.

GUMDROP CAKE

A plain cake, covered in lots of super-sweet frosting, and polka-dotted with candy, is perfect for a birthday celebration. · MAKES ONE 6-INCH ROUND CAKE (SERVES 4)

8 tablespoons unsalted butter,
    plus more for the pans
⅔ cup granulated sugar
2 large eggs
1 large egg yolk
2 teaspoons pure vanilla extract

⅓ cup heavy cream
1 cup cake flour
½ teaspoon baking powder
Pinch of salt
Frosting and Filling, recipe follows
Gumdrop slices, for finishing

Preheat the oven to 350°F. Butter the sides of two 6-inch round pans, and place a circle of parchment in the bottom of each pan. Set aside.

In the bowl of a stand mixer fitted with the paddle attachment, cream the remaining 8 tablespoons butter with the granulated sugar. Add the eggs, egg yolk, vanilla, and cream. Add the flour, baking powder, and salt, and mix just until combined. Divide the batter evenly between the prepared pans.

Bake until the edges start to brown and the centers are set, about 25 minutes. Cool for 10 minutes, then remove the cakes from the hot pans and cool completely on a wire rack. Using a serrated knife, trim off the dome of each cake and discard (or eat). Place one layer on a platter, bottom (flat) side up, and peel off the parchment round. Spread about one-third of the frosting and filling on top. Place the second layer on top, bottom (flat) side up, and peel off the parchment round. Spread the remaining frosting and filling on the top and sides and finish with a row of gumdrops "glued" around the cake.

FROSTING AND FILLING

20 tablespoons unsalted butter,
    softened
½ teaspoon pure vanilla extract
4 cups confectioners' sugar

¼ teaspoon salt
7 to 8 tablespoons heavy cream,
    as needed

recipe continues

In the bowl of a stand mixer fitted with the whisk attachment, mix the butter and vanilla. Add the confectioners' sugar and salt and whip until thickened. Add cream, as needed, to reach a spreadable consistency.

VARIATION: TRACEY CAKE
This lovely, old-fashioned cake is perfect for company. My children named it after me, because I make it all the time. For another variation, dress it up with jam, whipped cream, and berries, and you have a dessert that is similar to a Victoria sponge. · MAKES ONE 6-INCH ROUND CAKE (SERVES 4)

Gumdrop Cake, recipe on page 63   Fresh strawberries, for finishing
Chocolate Frosting and Filling,   Edible flowers, for finishing
   recipe follows

Follow the instructions for the layers of the Gumdrop Cake. Place a layer of the cooled cake on a platter, bottom (flat) side up. Peel off the parchment round. Cover with half of the Chocolate Frosting and Filling.

   Place the second cake layer on top, bottom (flat) side up. Peel off the parchment round. Cover the top with the remaining Chocolate Frosting and Filling, leaving the sides of the cake unfrosted.

   Finish with strawberries and edible flowers on top.

CHOCOLATE FROSTING AND FILLING
3 ounces bittersweet or   ¼ cup heavy cream, warmed
   semisweet chocolate, chopped   1 teaspoon pure vanilla extract
4 tablespoons unsalted butter   1 teaspoon light corn syrup
1 cup confectioners' sugar   Pinch of salt

In the top of a double boiler, melt the chocolate and butter. Whisk to combine and cool for 5 minutes off the heat.

   In the bowl of a stand mixer fitted with the whisk attachment, whip the chocolate-butter mixture, confectioners' sugar, cream, vanilla, corn syrup, and salt until thickened.

MY FAVORITE FLOURLESS CAKE

My wonderful friend Cara Tannenbaum has been cooking professionally for decades and is always available to help me test a cake, over and over, until perfection is achieved. She collaborated with me on this gem of a cake. I like to chill it, cut it into pieces, and then drip glaze on top. Alternatively, dust the cake with confectioners' sugar or serve it plain. • MAKES ONE 7-INCH ROUND CAKE (SERVES 4 TO 7)

4 tablespoons unsalted butter, plus more for the pan

4 ounces bittersweet or semisweet chocolate, chopped

1 teaspoon instant coffee granules (optional)

2 large eggs

Pinch of salt

½ cup granulated sugar

2 tablespoons Dutch process cocoa powder

¼ teaspoon pure vanilla extract

Chocolate Glaze, recipe follows (optional)

Preheat the oven to 350°F. Fill a large baking dish one-third of the way with very hot water and place in the oven. Butter the sides of a 7-inch heatproof glass bowl (such as Pyrex®) with straight sides. Place two 3 by 14-inch strips of parchment paper, crosswise, in the bowl, and then place a round of parchment paper in the bottom of the bowl, and set aside.

In the top of a double boiler, melt the remaining 4 tablespoons butter and the chocolate. Remove the top from the heat and let cool for 5 minutes. Add the instant coffee granules (if using), stir until combined, and set aside.

In the bowl of a stand mixer fitted with the whisk attachment, whip the eggs and salt. Gradually add the granulated sugar and whip until combined. Slowly add the melted butter-chocolate mixture, then the cocoa powder and whip until incorporated. Add the vanilla, and mix until combined. Scrape into

recipe continues

the prepared bowl, place the bowl in the water-filled baking dish, and bake until set, about 30 minutes. Remove the bowl from the water bath and let the cake cool completely in the bowl.

Place the bowl in the freezer for at least 3 hours. Use the ends of the parchment strips to lift the cake out of the bowl, remove the parchment strips and round, and cut the cake into eight pieces.

Line a half-sheet pan with parchment, and place a wire rack on top of the parchment. Place the cake pieces, separated, on top of the wire rack, and pour half of the glaze (if using) over them, frosting each piece separately. Let the cake sit for 10 minutes, then pour the remaining glaze over the pieces.

CHOCOLATE GLAZE

3 ounces bittersweet or semisweet
    chocolate, chopped

½ cup heavy cream
1 tablespoon light corn syrup

Place the chocolate in a heatproof bowl. Place the cream in a small saucepan, and heat just until bubbles form around the edges (do not boil). Pour the hot cream over the chocolate, let sit 5 minutes, then stir. Add the corn syrup and stir to combine until smooth.

MANGO CAKE

This sponge cake gets a hint of orange flavor from the liqueur. Try Grand Marnier or Cointreau. Garnishing it with mango and a few mint leaves makes for an unusual and lovely presentation. · MAKES ONE 4-INCH ROUND CAKE (SERVES 4)

4 tablespoons unsalted butter,
   plus more for the pans
⅓ cup granulated sugar
1 tablespoon packed light
   brown sugar
3 large eggs
1 tablespoon finely grated
   orange zest
1 teaspoon orange liqueur

1 teaspoon pure vanilla extract
½ cup all-purpose flour
¼ teaspoon salt
Whipped Cream with Orange
   Liqueur, recipe follows
½ ripe mango, peeled, pitted, and cut
   into matchsticks, for decorating
Mint leaves, for decorating

Preheat the oven to 350°F. Butter the sides of two 4-inch round cake pans, place a parchment round in the bottom of each, and set aside.

In the bowl of a stand mixer fitted with the paddle attachment, cream the remaining 4 tablespoons butter and the granulated and brown sugars. Add the eggs, mix to incorporate, then add the orange zest, orange liqueur, and vanilla and mix until incorporated. Add the flour and salt and mix just until combined.

Divide the batter evenly between the prepared pans and bake until set, about 20 minutes. Cool in the pans for 10 minutes, then remove the cakes from the hot pans and cool completely on a wire rack.

Using a serrated knife, trim off the dome of each cake and discard (or eat). Place one layer on a cake stand, bottom (flat) side up, and peel off the parchment round and discard.

Spread half of the whipped cream on top. Place the second layer on top, bottom (flat) side up, and peel off the parchment round. Transfer the remaining

recipe continues

whipped cream to a pastry bag fitted with a star tip and pipe it on the top of the cake (or simply spread it on if you prefer). Decoratively arrange the mango and mint leaves on top.

WHIPPED CREAM WITH ORANGE LIQUEUR

2 cups heavy cream

3 tablespoons granulated sugar

½ teaspoon orange liqueur

¼ teaspoon pure vanilla extract

⅛ teaspoon cream of tartar

Pinch of salt

In the bowl of a stand mixer fitted with the whisk attachment, start whipping the cream. As it thickens, gradually add the granulated sugar. Add the orange liqueur, vanilla, cream of tartar, and salt and whip until stiff peaks form.

LAMINGTONS

This amazing treat from Down Under will wow your guests. You will be surprised at how easy it is to whip up a little batch to make everyone happy.

• MAKES FOUR 4 BY 2-INCH CAKES (SERVES 4)

4 tablespoons unsalted butter,
  softened, plus more for the pan
⅓ cup granulated sugar
1 large egg
1 large egg yolk
1 teaspoon full-fat sour cream
1 teaspoon pure vanilla extract
¾ cup cake flour

Pinch of salt
2 ounces milk or dark chocolate,
  chopped
3 tablespoons heavy cream
1½ cups unsweetened shredded
  coconut
2 tablespoons raspberry jam
4 raspberries, for topping

Preheat the oven to 350°F. Butter an 8-inch square baking pan and set aside.

In the bowl of a stand mixer fitted with the paddle attachment, cream the remaining 4 tablespoons butter and the granulated sugar. Add the egg, egg yolk, sour cream, and vanilla and mix to incorporate. Add the flour and salt, and mix just until combined. Scrape into the prepared pan and bake until the edges start to brown and the center is set, about 13 minutes. Cool completely in the pan before removing the cake from the pan.

While the cake is cooling, place the chocolate and cream in the top of a double boiler. Gently whisk until the chocolate melts and the mixture is smooth. Pour into a heatproof bowl and let cool for 5 minutes.

Cut the cake into four 4-inch squares. Place the coconut in a medium bowl. Spread the jam on top of 2 squares. Place the 2 remaining squares on top of the jam-topped squares. With 2 forks, dip one cake into the chocolate, coating all sides, then lift the square with the forks and dip it into the coconut, coating all sides. Repeat with the remaining cake.

Place both squares on a platter in the refrigerator for 20 minutes before serving. Slice each square into two rectangles. Top each with a raspberry.

LEMON CAKE

This pretty cake has the bright flavor of lemon. · MAKES ONE 6-INCH ROUND
CAKE (SERVES 2 TO 4)

2 tablespoons unsalted butter,
   softened, plus more for the pan

Finely grated zest of 2 lemons

2 tablespoons granulated sugar

2 tablespoons packed light
   brown sugar

1 large egg

1 tablespoon heavy cream

1 teaspoon pure vanilla extract

¾ cup all-purpose flour

½ teaspoon baking powder

Pinch of salt

Lemon Glaze, recipe follows

Edible flower petals, for decorating

Preheat the oven to 350°F. Butter the sides of a 6-inch round baking pan, place a circle of parchment in the bottom of the pan, and set aside.

In the bowl of a stand mixer fitted with the paddle attachment, cream the remaining 2 tablespoons butter, the lemon zest, and granulated and brown sugars. Add the egg, cream, and vanilla and mix to incorporate. Add the flour, baking powder, and salt, and mix just until combined. Scrape into the prepared pan and bake until lightly browned on the edges, about 25 minutes. Cool in the pan for 10 minutes, then remove the cake from the hot pan and cool completely on a wire rack.

Pour the glaze on top of the cake in 3 additions, leaving about 10 minutes in between for the glaze to dry out a bit and set. If you don't, the glaze will puddle on the platter. Decorate the perimeter of the top of the cake with flower petals.

LEMON GLAZE

1½ cups confectioners' sugar, sifted

Finely grated zest of ½ lemon

2 to 3 tablespoons freshly squeezed
   lemon juice

Place the confectioners' sugar in a medium bowl and add the zest. Whisk in enough lemon juice to make a very thick glaze with no lumps.

MOCHA CAKE

Chocolate and coffee marry together perfectly, and studding the sweet frosting with chocolate pearls (or chips) is, as they say, "the icing on the cake."

• MAKES ONE 4-INCH ROUND CAKE (SERVES 2)

4 tablespoons unsalted butter, softened, plus more for the pans

2 tablespoons Dutch process cocoa powder

2 tablespoons boiling water

1 teaspoon instant coffee granules

¾ cup granulated sugar

1 tablespoon packed light brown sugar

1 large egg

2 tablespoons full-fat sour cream

2 teaspoons pure vanilla bean paste

½ cup cake flour

¼ teaspoon baking powder

⅛ teaspoon salt

Kahlúa Frosting, recipe follows

2 to 3 tablespoons chocolate pearls, for finishing

Preheat the oven to 350°F. Butter the sides of two 4-inch round cake pans, place a parchment round in the bottom of each, and set aside.

Combine the cocoa powder, boiling water, and coffee in a small bowl, and set aside to cool for 5 minutes. In the bowl of a stand mixer fitted with the paddle attachment, cream the remaining 4 tablespoons butter and the granulated and brown sugars. Add the egg, then the sour cream, vanilla bean paste, and cocoa-coffee mixture, beating to combine between additions. Add the flour, baking powder, and salt and mix just until combined.

Divide the batter evenly between the prepared pans. Bake for 30 minutes, or until set. Cool in the pans for 10 minutes, then remove the cakes from the hot pans and cool completely on a wire rack.

Using a serrated knife, trim off the dome of each cake and discard (or eat). Place one layer, bottom (flat) side up, on a platter, and peel off the parchment

recipe continues

round. Spread one-third of the frosting on top. Place the second layer on top, bottom (flat) side up, and peel off the parchment round.

Spread the remaining frosting on the top and sides of the cake, and finish by dotting the sides and top of the cake with the chocolate pearls.

KAHLÚA FROSTING

8 tablespoons unsalted butter, softened

1 teaspoon Kahlúa

¼ teaspoon pure vanilla extract

1½ cups confectioners' sugar

Pinch of salt

2 tablespoons heavy cream, or more as needed

In the clean bowl of a stand mixer fitted with the whisk attachment, whip the butter, Kahlúa, and vanilla. Add the confectioners' sugar, salt, and 2 tablespoons cream and whip until smooth and thickened. Whip in a bit more cream, if needed, to make a thick but spreadable frosting.

CARROT CAKE

In my opinion, the best carrot cakes are kitchen-sink mixtures, with pineapple, coconut, rum, dried fruit, and nuts, covered with a tangy cream cheese frosting. This recipe is my favorite version of this classic wintertime dessert.

• MAKES ONE 6-INCH RING CAKE (SERVES 4)

2 tablespoons unsalted butter, plus more for the pan

3 tablespoons fresh diced or canned crushed pineapple

¼ cup packed light brown sugar

2 tablespoons granulated sugar

1 large egg

1 tablespoon rum

¾ cup grated carrot

½ cup unsweetened shredded coconut

1 cup all-purpose flour

½ teaspoon ground cinnamon

½ teaspoon baking powder

¼ teaspoon baking soda

Pinch of salt

¼ cup walnut or pecan halves

¼ cup raisins

Cream Cheese Frosting, recipe follows

Edible flowers, for decorating

Preheat the oven to 350°F. Butter the sides and center tube of a 6-inch tube pan with removable bottom. Place a round of parchment, with a center hole cut out for the tube, in the bottom of the pan, and set aside.

If using canned pineapple, drain and discard the liquid.

In the bowl of a stand mixer fitted with the paddle attachment, cream the remaining 2 tablespoons butter, and the brown and granulated sugars. Add the egg and rum and beat to incorporate. Mix in the carrot, coconut, and pineapple. Add the flour, cinnamon, baking powder, baking soda, and salt, and mix just until combined. With a silicone spatula, fold in the nuts and raisins. Scrape into the prepared pan and bake until set, about 35 minutes. Cool completely in the pan. Remove the cake from the pan and remove the parchment. Spread the frosting on top of the cake, and decorate with edible flowers.

recipe continues

CREAM CHEESE FROSTING

4 ounces full-fat block cream cheese,
   softened
1½ tablespoons unsalted butter,
   softened

1 cup confectioners' sugar
½ teaspoon pure vanilla extract

In the bowl of a stand mixer fitted with the whisk attachment, whip the cream cheese and butter. Add the confectioners' sugar and whip to combine. Add the vanilla and whip until smooth.

QUAKE CAKE

Versions of this cake were popular about fifty years ago. I think it's time for the cake to make a comeback. As it cools, the top cracks and the center starts to cave in, as if there was an earthquake. The resulting confection isn't the prettiest, but it is truly delicious. Piping some whipped cream on top is a lovely touch.

• MAKES ONE 6-INCH ROUND CAKE (SERVES 4)

2 tablespoons unsalted butter, plus more for the pan

2 ounces bittersweet or semisweet chocolate, chopped

1 large egg yolk

¼ cup granulated sugar, divided

Pinch of salt

1 teaspoon Dutch process cocoa powder

2 large egg whites

¼ teaspoon pure vanilla extract

⅛ teaspoon cream of tartar

Whipped Cream, for finishing, recipe follows

Preheat the oven to 350°F. Butter the sides of a 6-inch springform pan and line the bottom with parchment paper. If your springform pan leaks, line the outside bottom and sides with aluminum foil, and set aside.

In the top of a double boiler, melt the remaining 2 tablespoons butter and the chopped chocolate. Whisk to combine and allow it to cool, off the heat, for 5 minutes.

In the bowl of a stand mixer fitted with the paddle attachment, beat the egg yolk, 2 tablespoons of the granulated sugar, and the salt. Slowly add the butter-chocolate mixture, then the cocoa powder, and mix until smooth. Transfer the mixture to a bowl and clean the mixer bowl. Place the clean mixer bowl on the stand mixer.

Fit the mixer with the whisk attachment and whip the egg whites, vanilla, and cream of tartar, until frothy. Slowly add the remaining 2 tablespoons of granulated sugar, and beat until stiff peaks form.

recipe continues

With a silicone spatula, gently fold the egg whites into the chocolate mixture, just until combined. Scrape into the prepared pan and bake until set, about 30 minutes. Cool for 10 minutes, then unbuckle and remove the sides of the hot pan, and cool the cake completely on the bottom of the pan set on a wire rack. Remove the cake from the base of the pan and discard the parchment paper.

Slice the cake, and pipe the whipped cream on top. Serve at room temperature, or place the cake in the refrigerator for an hour or more and serve chilled.

WHIPPED CREAM

½ cup heavy cream

¼ teaspoon pure vanilla extract

⅛ teaspoon cream of tartar

1 tablespoon plus 1½ teaspoons
   packed light brown sugar

In the bowl of a stand mixer fitted with the whisk attachment, whip the heavy cream and cream of tartar until frothy. Slowly add the brown sugar, then the vanilla, and whip until firm peaks form.

COFFEE CAKE

This cake does something curious in the oven. The filling placed on top of the batter sinks down into the cake while baking. It's an inside-out coffee cake, with a surprise inside each slice. · MAKES ONE 7-INCH RING CAKE (SERVES 4)

BATTER

6 tablespoons unsalted butter, softened, plus more for the pan

½ cup granulated sugar

¼ cup packed light brown sugar

2 large eggs

2 teaspoons pure vanilla extract

2 tablespoons full-fat sour cream

1 cup all-purpose flour

1 teaspoon baking powder

¼ teaspoon baking soda

Pinch of salt

FILLING

2 tablespoons packed light brown sugar

1 tablespoon granulated sugar

1 teaspoon ground cinnamon

3 tablespoons chocolate chips

2 tablespoons coarsely chopped pecans

1 tablespoon raisins

2 tablespoons unsalted butter, cold, cut into ¼-inch cubes

Confectioners' sugar, for dusting

Preheat the oven to 350°F. Butter the sides and center tube of a 7-inch tube pan with removable bottom, and place a circle of parchment, with a hole in the middle, on the bottom. Set aside.

In the bowl of a stand mixer fitted with the paddle attachment, cream the remaining 6 tablespoons butter and the granulated and brown sugars. Add the eggs, then the vanilla and sour cream and mix to incorporate. Add the flour, baking powder, baking soda, and salt and mix just until combined. Scrape into the prepared pan and set aside.

Make the filling in a medium bowl: Toss together the brown and granulated sugars and cinnamon. Add the chocolate chips, pecans, raisins, and butter, and toss, coating the butter.

recipe continues

Place the filling on top of the batter, avoiding the sides and center tube of the pan. Bake until set, about 40 minutes. Cool for 15 minutes, then, pushing from the bottom of the pan, remove the sides of the pan (be careful, the pan might still be hot).

Cool completely on the pan bottom set on a wire rack. When the cake is cool, remove the pan bottom and discard the parchment paper. Dust the cake with confectioners' sugar just before serving.

FINANCIERS

These little cakes are traditionally made in bars to resemble gold ingots. Although they are made with ground almonds, they have a hazelnut aroma when warm, which comes from heating the butter until just golden to make what is known as *beurre noisette*. You can be creative with this recipe, substituting any other nut flour, such as hazelnut or pistachio, for the almond flour or even adding grated chocolate. I found a few bakeries in France that bake financiers with confectioners' sugar, but I prefer granulated. Some also bake a tiny nut or piece of dried fruit inside, but financiers are best eaten plain, or with a dab of cherry preserves on top. I like to bake them in metal pans, but there are also silicone and metal molds to make small cakes in all sorts of delightful shapes, if you prefer.

• MAKES TWO 2½ BY 3¾-INCH CAKES OR MORE SMALLER CAKES

4 tablespoons unsalted butter, plus
   more for the pan
2 large egg whites
¼ cup granulated sugar
⅓ cup ground almond flour
2 tablespoons cake flour

Pinch of baking powder
Pinch of salt
½ teaspoon pure vanilla extract
Confectioners' sugar, for dusting
   (optional)

Preheat the oven to 350°F. Butter two 2½ by 3¾-inch wells of a financier pan, and set aside.

In a medium saucepan, melt the remaining 4 tablespoons butter, gently whisking until it just begins to brown on the edges. You don't want it to darken or burn. Immediately remove the pan from the heat, pour the butter into a heat-proof bowl, and let cool for 10 minutes.

In the bowl of a stand mixer fitted with the whisk attachment, whip the egg whites until frothy. Gradually add the granulated sugar, then the almond and cake flours, baking powder, and salt. Add the vanilla and melted butter, and mix

recipe continues

just until combined. Scrape the batter into the prepared pan, filling the wells three-quarters full.

Bake until browned and set, about 25 minutes. Let cool for 5 minutes in the pan, then remove the cakes from the hot pan, cool for a few minutes on a wire rack, and serve warm. Or let the cakes cool completely and dust with confectioners' sugar (if using) before serving.

CHAPTER

№ 3

SPRING

SPRINKLE CAKES

During my childhood, local sweet shops in my native Massachusetts added chocolate or rainbow sprinkles to scoops of ice cream. In college, I called the rainbow sprinkles "Valeries" in honor of a sweet (pun intended) fellow student. Everyone on our dorm floor called them that, too—I hope they still do. These cakes are for her.

• MAKES THREE 3-INCH BUNDT CAKES (SERVES 3)

4 tablespoons unsalted butter,
   softened, plus more for the pan

½ cup granulated sugar, divided

¼ cup heavy cream

Finely grated zest of 1 orange

1 teaspoon pure vanilla extract

¾ cup cake flour

½ teaspoon baking powder

Pinch of salt

2 large egg whites

⅛ teaspoon cream of tartar

2 tablespoons colored sprinkles

Chocolate Drizzle, recipe follows

Nonpareils or more sprinkles,
   for finishing

Preheat the oven to 350°F. Butter three wells of a Bundt cakelet pan and set the pan aside.

In the bowl of a stand mixer fitted with the paddle attachment, cream the remaining 4 tablespoons butter and ¼ cup of the granulated sugar. Add the heavy cream, orange zest, and vanilla. Add the flour, baking powder, and salt and mix just until combined. Transfer this mixture to a medium bowl and set aside. Clean the mixer bowl.

In the clean bowl of the stand mixer fitted with the whisk attachment, whip the egg whites and cream of tartar until frothy. Slowly add the remaining ¼ cup granulated sugar and whip until stiff peaks form.

With a silicone spatula, gently fold the sprinkles and the egg white mixture into the cake batter, just until combined. Divide the batter evenly among

recipe continues

the wells of the prepared pan, and bake until the edges start to lightly brown and the cakes are set, about 20 minutes. Cool in the pan for 10 minutes, then remove the cakes from the pan and cool completely on a wire rack.

Top with the chocolate drizzle and decorate with nonpareils.

CHOCOLATE DRIZZLE

1½ ounces bittersweet or semisweet
    chocolate, chopped

¼ cup heavy cream

1 teaspoon light corn syrup

Place the chocolate in a heatproof bowl. In a small saucepan, heat the cream just until bubbles form around the edges (do not boil). Pour the cream over the chocolate, let sit for 5 minutes, then mix. Add the corn syrup and mix until smooth.

CHERRY CAKES

These pretty little cakes, made in fluted tart pans, are a light and refreshing spring or summer dessert. I once had a piece of a similar cake in France that had un-pitted cherries baked in, but I always pit cherries unless they are going to be displayed on the top with their stems intact. · MAKES FOUR 4-INCH ROUND CAKES (SERVES 4)

4 tablespoons unsalted butter,
   softened, plus more for the pans
⅓ cup granulated sugar,
   plus more for sprinkling
1 large egg yolk
¼ cup heavy cream
1 cup all-purpose flour
1 teaspoon baking powder

¼ teaspoon salt
14 cherries, stemmed,
   pitted, and halved
Whipped Cream, for finishing,
   recipe follows
4 whole cherries with stems,
   for finishing

Preheat the oven to 350°F. Butter the bottoms and sides of four 4-inch tart pans with removable bottoms. Line a half-sheet pan with parchment paper and set the pans aside.

In the bowl of a stand mixer fitted with the paddle attachment, cream the remaining 4 tablespoons butter and ⅓ cup granulated sugar. Add the egg yolk and cream and beat to incorporate. Add the flour, baking powder, and salt, and mix just until combined. The batter will be somewhat stiff.

Divide the batter evenly among the prepared tart pans, smooth the batter, and place 7 cherry halves, cut sides down, on top in a single layer. Push the cherries part of the way into the batter, and sprinkle some granulated sugar on top of the fruit.

Place the tart pans on the prepared half-sheet pan, making sure they don't touch one another. Bake until the edges start to brown and some of the juice from the cherries starts to bubble, about 25 minutes.

recipe continues

Cool for 10 minutes, then remove the sides of the pans (careful, they will still be very hot).

Continue to cool the cakes completely on the bottoms of the hot pans on a wire rack, and remove the bottoms before serving. Finish each cake by adding a dollop of whipped cream and a fresh cherry on top.

WHIPPED CREAM

½ cup heavy cream

⅛ teaspoon cream of tartar

1 tablespoon plus 1½ teaspoons packed
   light brown sugar

½ teaspoon pure vanilla extract

In the bowl of a stand mixer fitted with the whisk attachment, whip the heavy cream and cream of tartar until frothy. Slowly add the brown sugar, then the vanilla, and whip until firm peaks form.

PISTACHIO CHERRY CAKE

This lovely cake is traditionally finished with frosting. It often has strawberries, but I love the combination of almond flavoring, cherries, and pistachio or berry dust. I make it for my son Willie, who prefers cakes like this with lots of frosting.

• MAKES ONE 4-INCH ROUND CAKE (SERVES 4)

4 tablespoons unsalted butter, softened, plus more for the pan

¼ cup granulated sugar

1 tablespoon packed light brown sugar

1 large egg

3 tablespoons heavy cream

1 teaspoon pure vanilla extract

¼ teaspoon pure almond extract

1 cup all-purpose flour

1 teaspoon baking powder

Pinch of salt

Vanilla-Almond Frosting, recipe follows

1 cup stemmed and pitted cherries

Pistachio Dust or Strawberry Dust, for finishing, recipe follows

4 whole cherries with stems, for finishing

Preheat the oven to 350°F. Butter the sides of two 4-inch round pans, and place a round of parchment paper in the bottom of each pan. Set aside.

In the bowl of a stand mixer fitted with the paddle attachment, cream the remaining 4 tablespoons butter and the granulated and brown sugars. Add the egg, then the cream, and then the vanilla and almond extracts, beating to combine between additions. Add the flour, baking powder, and salt and mix just until combined. Divide evenly between the prepared pans and bake until lightly browned and set, about 30 minutes.

Cool for 10 minutes in the pans, then remove the cakes from the hot pans and cool completely on a wire rack.

recipe continues

Using a serrated knife, trim off the dome of each cake and discard (or eat). Place a layer of cake on a platter, bottom (flat) side up, and peel off the parchment round. Spread about one-third of the frosting on top and scatter the pitted cherries on top. Place the second layer of cake on top, bottom (flat) side up, and peel off the parchment round. Spread the remaining frosting on the top and sides of the cake.

Press the pistachio or berry dust around the bottom of the cake, coming up about one-quarter of the cake, and on top of the cake. Finish by placing the whole cherries with stems on top of the cake.

VANILLA-ALMOND FROSTING

4 tablespoons unsalted butter, softened

⅛ teaspoon pure almond extract

1 cup confectioners' sugar

About 2 tablespoons heavy cream, or more as needed

Pinch of salt

In the bowl of a stand mixer fitted with the whisk attachment, whip the butter, almond extract, confectioners' sugar, 2 tablespoons cream, and salt. Whip until thickened, adding a bit more cream, if needed, to reach a spreadable consistency.

PISTACHIO OR STRAWBERRY DUST

¼ cup granulated sugar

¼ cup unsalted pistachios or freeze-dried strawberries

In the bowl of a food processor fitted with the metal blade, pulse the granulated sugar and pistachios until the nuts are coarsely ground. If using the strawberries, pulse them with the granulated sugar into a fine dust.

CHOCOLATE BIRTHDAY CAKE

For our family birthday cake, I double the size of the layers, triple the chocolate frosting (for my daughter-in-law Marki) and meringue filling (for David, my husband), and stick a chopstick or two straight down to keep the top layer from sliding onto the floor. · MAKES ONE 6-INCH ROUND CAKE (SERVES 4)

8 tablespoons unsalted butter,
    softened, plus more for the pans
¼ cup Dutch process cocoa powder
¼ cup heavy cream
¾ cup granulated sugar
1 tablespoon packed light
    brown sugar
2 large eggs
¼ cup full-fat sour cream
2 teaspoons pure vanilla bean paste

1 cup cake flour
½ teaspoon baking powder
¼ teaspoon baking soda
¼ teaspoon salt
Swiss Meringue Filling,
    recipe follows
Strawberries, some hulled and
    sliced in half and some whole
    with stems, for finishing
Chocolate Frosting, recipe follows

Preheat the oven to 350°F. Butter the sides of two 6-inch round cake pans and place a parchment round in the bottom of each. Set aside.

In the top of a double boiler, heat the cocoa powder and cream until bubbles begin to form around the edges, while gently stirring. Remove the top from the heat, and cool for 5 minutes.

In the bowl of a stand mixer fitted with the paddle attachment, cream the remaining 8 tablespoons butter and the granulated and brown sugars. Beat in the eggs, then the sour cream, the vanilla bean paste, and the cocoa-cream mixture. Add the flour, baking powder, baking soda, and salt and mix just until combined.

Divide the batter equally between the prepared pans. Bake for 25 minutes, or until set. Cool in the pans for 10 minutes, then remove the cakes from the hot pans, and cool completely on a wire rack. Using a serrated knife, trim off the dome of each cake and discard (or eat). Place a layer of cake on a platter, bottom (flat) side up, and peel off the parchment round.

recipe continues

Spread the meringue filling on top and place strawberry halves on the filling. Place the second layer on top, bottom (flat) side up, and peel off the parchment round. Spread the frosting on top, and finish with whole strawberries.

SWISS MERINGUE FILLING

3 large egg whites
1 cup plus 1 tablespoon
  granulated sugar

Pinch of cream of tartar
Pinch of salt
½ teaspoon pure vanilla extract

Place the egg whites and granulated sugar in the metal bowl of your stand mixer. Place the bowl over a saucepan of boiling water, creating a double boiler, making sure the bottom of the bowl does not touch the water. With a wire whisk, continuously whisk the mixture until it reaches 165°F. Remove the bowl from the saucepan (be careful, it will be hot), and, with a paper towel, wipe the bottom of the bowl. Place the bowl on the stand mixer fitted with the whisk attachment and whip until soft peaks form. Add the cream of tartar and salt, and whip until stiff peaks form and the filling cools. Whip in the vanilla until incorporated.

CHOCOLATE FROSTING

3 ounces bittersweet or semisweet
  chocolate, chopped
4 tablespoons unsalted butter
1 cup confectioners' sugar

¼ cup heavy cream, warmed
2 teaspoons pure vanilla bean paste
1 teaspoon light corn syrup
Pinch of salt

In the top of a double boiler, melt the chocolate and butter. Whisk to combine, remove from the heat, and cool for 5 minutes. In the bowl of a stand mixer fitted with the whisk attachment, whip the chocolate-butter mixture, confectioners' sugar, cream, vanilla bean paste, corn syrup, and salt until thickened.

CHOCOLATE CHIP CUPCAKES
with choice of two frostings

My grandson, Brody, doesn't like most sweets but he will occasionally share a cupcake with me, his Nonna Honey. This recipe makes a small batch of these dainty treats. • MAKES FOUR CUPCAKES (SERVES 2)

4 tablespoons unsalted butter, softened

⅓ cup granulated sugar

1 large egg

2 tablespoons full-fat sour cream

½ teaspoon pure vanilla extract

½ cup all-purpose flour

¼ teaspoon baking powder

Pinch of salt

⅓ cup chocolate chips

Chocolate Whipped Cream Frosting, recipe follows

Vanilla Frosting, recipe follows

Nonpareils, for finishing

Preheat the oven to 350°F. Place four cupcake papers in the wells of a cupcake pan and set aside.

In the bowl of a stand mixer fitted with the paddle attachment, cream the butter and granulated sugar. Add the egg and beat until incorporated, then add the sour cream and vanilla and beat until incorporated. Add the flour, baking powder, and salt and mix just until combined.

With a silicone spatula, fold in the chocolate chips. With a #24 (2.7-tablespoon) spring-loaded scoop, fill the cupcake papers. Bake until set, about 25 minutes. Cool completely in the pan before removing the cupcakes from the pan.

With an offset metal spatula, spread each type of frosting on two cupcakes, then sprinkle nonpareils on top.

recipe continues

CHOCOLATE WHIPPED CREAM FROSTING FOR TWO CUPCAKES

2 ounces bittersweet or semisweet chocolate, chopped

Pinch of salt

¼ cup heavy cream

Place the chocolate and salt in the metal bowl of your stand mixer. In a small saucepan, heat the cream until bubbles appear around the edges (don't boil), and pour over the chocolate in the bowl. Let the mixture sit for 5 minutes, then mix until completely combined. Leave the bowl on your work surface and let the mixture cool completely. Fit the stand mixer with the whisk attachment, and whip the mixture until medium peaks form. Do not overwhip the frosting, as it can become grainy.

VANILLA FROSTING FOR TWO CUPCAKES

2 ounces full-fat block cream cheese, softened

3 tablespoons unsalted butter, softened

¼ teaspoon pure vanilla extract

1 cup confectioners' sugar

In the bowl of a stand mixer fitted with the whisk attachment, whip the cream cheese, butter, and vanilla until combined. Add the confectioners' sugar, and whip until smooth.

CHECKERBOARD CAKES

This cake is a cousin to the Battenberg, which is made with pink and yellow cake and wrapped in rolled marzipan instead of frosting. Rather than raspberry jam, you can use your favorite preserves or marmalade in between the layers.

• MAKES TWO 8-INCH LOAF CAKES (SERVES 8)

6 tablespoons unsalted butter, softened, plus more for the pans

¾ cup granulated sugar

2 large eggs

½ cup full-fat sour cream

1 teaspoon pure vanilla extract

1½ cups all-purpose flour

1½ teaspoons baking powder

Pinch of salt

¼ cup Dutch process cocoa powder, plus more for dusting

¼ cup plus 1 tablespoon boiling water

¼ cup plus 2 tablespoons raspberry jam, for finishing

Chocolate Frosting, recipe follows

Preheat the oven to 350°F. Butter two 8-inch square baking pans and set aside.

In the bowl of a stand mixer fitted with the paddle attachment, cream the remaining 6 tablespoons butter with the granulated sugar. Add the eggs and beat until incorporated, then add the sour cream and vanilla and beat until incorporated. Add the flour, baking powder, and salt, and mix just until combined. Scrape a little more than half the batter into one of the prepared pans. Keep the paddle attachment on the mixer.

Return the bowl with the remaining batter to the mixer.

In a small bowl, combine the ¼ cup cocoa powder and boiling water and mix well with a silicone spatula. Add the cocoa mixture to the remaining batter, and mix just until combined.

Scrape the batter into the second prepared pan. Bake both cakes until set, about 25 minutes. Cool completely in the pans before removing the cakes from the pans.

recipe continues

Trim the edges of each cake. Cut each cake to make four rectangular pieces, eight pieces total (four of each flavor), that are identical in size and shape—about 2 by 8 inches each.

Place one piece of chocolate cake on top of a piece of parchment paper. Spread the top of the cake with a small amount of the jam, and place a piece of vanilla cake on top. Leaving a few inches of space, place a piece of vanilla cake next to the first chocolate piece, spread with more of the jam, then place another piece of chocolate cake on top. Place more of the jam between the two double layers of cake, and gently press them together, making a checkerboard.

Repeat with the remaining four pieces to make a second checkerboard. Place the cakes in the freezer for 10 minutes to firm up while preparing the frosting.

Place one cake on a platter with 2 fresh strips of parchment paper under the long edges. Repeat with the second cake on a different platter with more parchment. Using an offset metal spatula, frost the tops and long sides of each cake, leaving the short sides open so that you can see the checkerboard pattern. Trim the short sides, if necessary, and slip out the parchment paper and discard.

Refrigerate the cakes for 45 minutes to allow the preserves to set and stick the cake layers together. Dust with cocoa powder before serving.

CHOCOLATE FROSTING

4 ounces bittersweet or semisweet chocolate, chopped	Pinch of salt
	½ cup heavy cream

Place the chocolate and salt in the metal bowl of your stand mixer. In a small saucepan, heat the cream just until bubbles form around the edges (do not boil) and pour over the chocolate in the bowl. Let the mixture sit for 5 minutes, then mix until completely combined. Leave the bowl on your work surface to let the frosting cool completely. Fit the stand mixer with the whisk attachment, and whip the mixture until medium peaks form. Do not overwhip, as the frosting can become grainy.

PINEAPPLE-COCONUT CAKE

Pineapple and coconut are two flavors that marry perfectly, making one lovely cake. · MAKES ONE 4-INCH ROUND CAKE (SERVES 4)

2 tablespoons unsalted butter,
softened, plus more for the pan

¼ cup granulated sugar

2 tablespoons packed
light brown sugar

1 large egg

3 tablespoons fresh, diced pineapple
or 3 tablespoons canned
crushed pineapple in syrup
plus 1 teaspoon syrup

2 tablespoons vanilla yogurt or
full-fat sour cream

1 teaspoon rum

1 teaspoon pure vanilla extract

½ cup unsweetened shredded
coconut, lightly toasted

1 teaspoon chopped candied
orange peel

½ cup all-purpose flour

½ teaspoon baking powder

Pinch of salt

Cream Cheese Frosting, recipe follows

1 large edible flower, for finishing

Preheat the oven to 350°F. Butter the sides of two 4-inch round pans, place a circle of parchment in the bottom of each pan, and set aside.

In the bowl of a stand mixer fitted with the paddle attachment, cream the remaining 2 tablespoons butter with the granulated and brown sugars. Add the egg, pineapple (plus 1 teaspoon of syrup, if using canned), yogurt, rum, and vanilla and beat to incorporate. Add the coconut and orange peel and mix until combined. Add the flour, baking powder, and salt and mix just until combined.

Divide the batter evenly between the prepared pans. Bake until the edges start to brown, about 25 minutes. Cool for 10 minutes in the pans, then remove the cake layers from the hot pans and cool completely on a wire rack.

Using a serrated knife, trim off the dome of each cake and discard (or eat). Place one layer on a platter, bottom (flat) side up, and peel off the parchment

recipe continues

round. Spread half of the frosting on top. Place the second layer of cake on top, bottom (flat) side up, and peel off the parchment round. With an offset spatula, spread the remaining frosting on the top and a light coating on the sides of the cake, and finish with the edible flower on top.

CREAM CHEESE FROSTING

4 ounces full-fat block cream cheese, softened

1½ tablespoons unsalted butter, softened

¾ teaspoon pure vanilla extract

1 cup confectioners' sugar

In the bowl of a stand mixer fitted with the whisk attachment, whip the cream cheese, butter, and vanilla until incorporated. Add the confectioners' sugar, and whip until smooth.

FUDGY CAKE

Here's a little dessert that is just one layer. It doesn't need much on top, just some whipped cream. · MAKES ONE 6-INCH ROUND CAKE (SERVES 4)

4 tablespoons unsalted butter,
   plus more for the pan
2 ounces bittersweet or semisweet
   chocolate, chopped
1 large egg
¼ cup granulated sugar
Pinch of salt

1 tablespoon Dutch process
   cocoa powder
1 teaspoon rum or orange liqueur
½ teaspoon pure vanilla extract
Whipped Cream, recipe follows,
   for topping
1 goldenberry

Preheat the oven to 350°F. Fill a large baking dish one-third of the way with very hot water and place in the oven. Butter the sides of a 6-inch heatproof glass bowl (such as Pyrex®) with straight sides. Place two 3 by 14-inch strips of parchment, crosswise, in the bowl, and then place a circle of parchment on the bottom of the bowl. Set aside.

In the top of a double boiler, melt the remaining 4 tablespoons butter and the chocolate. Remove the top from the heat and let cool for 5 minutes.

In the bowl of a stand mixer fitted with the whisk attachment, whip the egg. Slowly add the granulated sugar, then the salt, and mix until combined. Add the melted butter-chocolate mixture, then the cocoa powder, and mix until combined. Add the rum and vanilla and mix until combined. Scrape into the prepared bowl and carefully place the bowl in the water-filled dish in the oven.

Bake until set, about 35 minutes. Remove the bowl from the water bath and cool in the bowl for 10 minutes. Use the ends of the parchment strips to lift the

recipe continues

cake out of the bowl, and remove the circle of parchment. Cool completely on a wire rack.

Spread the whipped cream on the cooled cake, and top with the goldenberry.

WHIPPED CREAM

½ cup heavy cream
⅛ teaspoon cream of tartar

2 tablespoons packed light
   brown sugar
¼ teaspoon pure vanilla bean paste

In the bowl of a stand mixer fitted with the whisk attachment, whip the cream and cream of tartar until frothy. Slowly add the brown sugar, then the vanilla bean paste, and whip until firm peaks form.

CHOCOLATE CHIP MADELEINES

Marcel Proust, in *Remembrance of Things Past*, rhapsodized about these sweet little madeleines, which he always dipped in tea. When I make them, I think of Ludwig Bemelmans's "twelve little girls in two straight lines . . . The smallest one was Madeline," and wonder if they ate these cakes. However you spell it, dipped in tea or not, these chocolate chip treats will delight.

• MAKES FOUR 3-INCH CAKES (SERVES 2)

1 tablespoon unsalted butter, melted, plus more for the pan
1 tablespoon granulated sugar
1 teaspoon packed light brown sugar
1 large egg yolk
1 teaspoon heavy cream

¼ teaspoon pure vanilla extract
¼ cup all-purpose flour
¼ teaspoon baking powder
Pinch of salt
2 teaspoons chocolate chips
Confectioners' sugar, for dusting

Preheat the oven to 350°F. Butter four wells of a madeleine pan and set aside.

In the bowl of a stand mixer fitted with the paddle attachment, mix the melted butter, granulated and brown sugars, egg yolk, cream, and vanilla. Add the flour, baking powder, and salt and mix just until combined.

Divide evenly among the wells of the prepared pan. Add a few chocolate chips to each, and bake until the edges start to brown and the centers are set, about 13 minutes.

Cool in the pan for 5 minutes, then remove the cakes from the hot pan and cool completely on a wire rack. Dust with confectioners' sugar before serving.

BLONDIES

As the only girl in a large family of boys, I was always in charge of the little kids. Sometimes, after a meal, to get all those children out of the house, my Sicilian grandfather presented me with a precious quarter or two. My brothers and I would march to the local store. This was no democracy—I was the decider of how that money would be spent. Candy, gum, or a miniature pie? Or five little snack cakes, no sharing required? The cakes usually won out. Once in a while, I chose these sweet squares as an alternative to my beloved brownies. They are caramel-y, chewy, and easy to make. Kids love finding a few, wrapped in waxed paper, tucked into their lunchboxes. • MAKES SIXTEEN 2-INCH SQUARES (SERVES 8)

8 tablespoons unsalted butter, softened, plus more for the pan

1 cup packed light brown sugar

1 large egg

1½ teaspoons pure vanilla extract

1 cup all-purpose flour

1 teaspoon baking powder

Pinch of salt

½ cup chocolate chips, plus more for topping batter

½ cup pecan or walnut halves, plus more for topping batter

Preheat the oven to 350°F. Butter an 8-inch square pan and set aside.

In the bowl of a stand mixer fitted with the paddle attachment, cream the remaining 8 tablespoons butter and the brown sugar. Add the egg and vanilla and beat to combine. Add the flour, baking powder, and salt and mix just until combined. With a silicone spatula, fold in the ½ cup chocolate chips and ½ cup nuts. Scrape into the prepared pan, and sprinkle a few more chocolate chips and nuts on top.

Bake until the cake starts to brown, about 30 minutes. Cool completely in the pan, remove the cake from the pan, and cut into 2-inch squares.

CHEESECAKE WITH CHERRY SAUCE

Dotty, an old friend of my mother's, taught me to make this delightful dessert when I was young. Often, I use amaretti, chocolate chip, or icebox cookies for the crust, instead of the expected graham crackers. I added the cherries in syrup for an elegant presentation. · MAKES ONE 6-INCH ROUND CAKE (SERVES 4 TO 6)

COOKIE OR GRAHAM CRACKER CRUST

2 tablespoons butter, melted,
　plus more for the pan
½ cup finely ground amaretti,
　chocolate chip cookies, icebox
　cookies, or graham crackers

2 tablespoons granulated sugar
1 tablespoon finely grated orange zest
　(optional)

Preheat the oven to 350°F. Butter the sides of a 6-inch springform pan and place a round of parchment in the bottom. Set aside.

　Place the melted butter, cookies, granulated sugar, and orange zest (if using) in the bowl of a food processor fitted with the metal blade. Pulse to combine. Press this mixture onto the bottom and ½ inch up the side of the prepared pan and set aside. Rinse the bowl and blade of the food processor, and return them to the machine.

recipe continues

CHEESECAKE FILLING

8 ounces full-fat block cream cheese,
   softened

¼ cup granulated sugar

¼ cup full-fat sour cream

1 large egg

½ teaspoon pure vanilla extract

Pinch of salt

Amarena cherries in syrup,
   for finishing

Place the cream cheese, granulated sugar, sour cream, egg, vanilla, and salt in the bowl of the food processor fitted with the metal blade and pulse until combined and lump-free. Pour this mixture on top of the crust in the prepared pan.

Bake just until the edges start to brown and the center is set, about 30 minutes. Cracks in the top of the cake are to be expected. Cool for 10 minutes, then unbuckle and remove the sides of the pan (be careful, it will still be very hot).

Cool the cake completely on the bottom of the pan, and chill for about 30 minutes before removing the bottom of the pan and the parchment paper. Finish by pouring amarena cherries and some of their syrup on top of the cake.

CHAPTER

№ 4

SUMMER

CHOCOLATE ROLL

Back in the mid-twentieth century, Dione Lucas and Paula Peck were baking icons. Decades later, their books taught me to make a simple, delicate chocolate sponge cake—the ancestor of this chocolate roll. I like to sprinkle colorful candy quins (short for sequins) on top. • MAKES ONE 8-INCH ROLL (SERVES 4)

4 ounces bittersweet or semisweet
   chocolate, chopped

4 large eggs, separated

½ cup granulated sugar, divided

1 tablespoon finely grated orange zest

⅛ teaspoon cream of tartar

Pinch of salt

2 tablespoons raspberry or cherry
   preserves, for finishing

Cinnamon-scented Whipped Cream,
   recipe follows

12 raspberries, for finishing

Ganache, recipe follows

Quins, for sprinkling

Preheat the oven to 350°F. Line a quarter sheet pan with parchment paper and set aside.

In the top of a double boiler, melt the chocolate. Remove the top from the heat and let cool for 10 minutes.

In the bowl of a stand mixer fitted with the paddle attachment, mix the 4 yolks, ¼ cup of the granulated sugar, and the orange zest until the mixture is thickened and light in color. Fold in the cooled melted chocolate and set aside.

In the clean bowl of your stand mixer fitted with the whisk attachment, mix the 4 egg whites, cream of tartar, and salt until foamy. Slowly add the remaining ¼ cup granulated sugar and beat until stiff peaks form. With a silicone spatula, gently fold the whites into the chocolate batter.

Gently spread the batter in an even layer on the prepared pan, and bake until set, about 15 minutes. Spread a clean, damp flatweave kitchen towel on top of the cake and cool completely in the pan.

recipe continues

Remove the kitchen towel and spread the preserves on the cooled cake in an even layer. Spread about two thirds of the whipped cream on top of the preserves, then sprinkle raspberries on top of the whipped cream. Roll up the cake like you would a jelly roll, using the parchment. Place the cake wrapped in parchment, seam side down, on a sheet pan and refrigerate for 15 minutes. Discard the parchment. Spread the ganache over the cake, then pipe the remaining whipped cream on top of the cake, and sprinkle with quins.

GANACHE

4 ounces dark chocolate, chopped   2 tablespoons light corn syrup

6 tablespoons heavy cream

Place the chocolate in a medium heatproof bowl and set aside.

Place the cream in a small saucepan and heat just until bubbles form around the edges (do not boil).

Pour the hot cream over the chocolate, let sit for 10 minutes, then stir. Add the corn syrup and stir until smooth.

CINNAMON-SCENTED WHIPPED CREAM

¾ cup heavy cream   ¼ teaspoon ground cinnamon

⅛ teaspoon cream of tartar   ½ teaspoon pure vanilla extract

2 tablespoons granulated sugar

In the bowl of a stand mixer fitted with the whisk attachment, whip the cream and cream of tartar until soft peaks form. Slowly add the granulated sugar and cinnamon, then the vanilla, and whip until stiff peaks form.

BLACKBERRY POPPY SEED CAKE

This cake is yummy and bursting with gorgeous fresh berries. You can also substitute raspberries or pitted, stemmed cherries for the blackberries. My fellow baker Jenny's sweet glaze adds beautiful color to this cake. · MAKES ONE 5-INCH BUNDT CAKE (SERVES 4)

3 tablespoons unsalted butter, softened, plus more for the pan

¼ cup granulated sugar, plus more for the pan

⅓ cup vanilla yogurt or full-fat sour cream

1 large egg

Finely grated zest of 1 lemon

2 tablespoons poppy seeds

½ cup all-purpose flour

½ teaspoon baking powder

Pinch of salt

½ cup blackberries, plus more for topping

Jenny's Glaze, recipe follows

Edible dried violets, for finishing

Preheat the oven to 350°F. Butter one 5-inch well of a Bundt quartet pan. Sprinkle some granulated sugar into the well, shake to coat, and discard the excess sugar.

In the bowl of a stand mixer fitted with the paddle attachment, cream the remaining 3 tablespoons butter with the remaining ¼ cup granulated sugar. Add the yogurt, egg, and lemon zest and beat to combine. Add the poppy seeds and beat to incorporate. Add the flour, baking powder, and salt and mix just until combined. With a silicone spatula, gently fold in the ½ cup blackberries.

Scrape into the prepared pan and bake until the edges are lightly browned and the cake is set, about 30 minutes. Cool for 10 minutes in the pan, then remove the cake from the hot pan and cool completely on a wire rack. Drizzle the glaze on top, and finish with dried violets and a few blackberries.

recipe continues

JENNY'S GLAZE

¾ cup blackberries   ½ cup confectioners' sugar
Juice of 1 lemon

In a food processor fitted with the metal blade, pulse the blackberries and lemon juice. In a small bowl, mix the confectioners' sugar and 2 tablespoons of the blackberry-lemon mixture to make a thick glaze.

If you prefer a seedless glaze, strain the mixture through a fine-mesh sieve.

BLUEBERRY CAKE

Here is the perfect treat to have with a cup of tea or a glass of milk. For the last forty years, my neighbors at the beach have picked the tiny local blueberries for baking and summer snacking. However, I prefer the big, juicy blueberries from the farmers' market for this delicious little cake. · MAKES ONE 5-INCH BUNDT CAKE (SERVES 4)

3 tablespoons unsalted butter, softened, plus more for the pan

¼ cup plus 2 tablespoons granulated sugar, plus more for the pan

1 large egg yolk

⅓ cup full-fat sour cream

½ teaspoon pure vanilla extract

½ cup all-purpose flour

½ teaspoon baking powder

Pinch of salt

¼ cup blueberries

Confectioners' sugar, for dusting

Preheat the oven to 350°F. Butter one 5-inch well of a quartet Bundt pan. Sprinkle some granulated sugar into the pan, shake to coat, and discard the excess. Set aside.

In the bowl of a stand mixer fitted with the paddle attachment, cream the remaining 3 tablespoons butter with the remaining ¼ cup plus 2 tablespoons granulated sugar. Add the egg yolk and beat to incorporate, then add the sour cream and vanilla, beating to incorporate. Add the flour, baking powder and salt and mix just until combined. With a silicone spatula, fold in the blueberries.

Scrape the batter into the prepared pan and smooth the top with the back of a spoon. Bake until lightly browned and set, about 35 minutes. Cool for 10 minutes in the pan, then remove the cake from the hot pan and cool completely on a wire rack. Just before serving, dust with confectioners' sugar.

EVERYTHING CAKE

Here are three ways to make this one amazing cake, using the same brownie-like batter and different toppings. At room temperature, the cake part is almost fudgelike. I prefer to pop it into the refrigerator after cooling for a slightly firmer consistency. I make a version with chocolate chips and peanut butter cups for my son Ben, who loves chocolate and peanut butter. • MAKES ONE 8-INCH SQUARE CAKE (SERVES 4)

BATTER

8 tablespoons unsalted butter

2 ounces bittersweet or semisweet
  chocolate, chopped

1 tablespoon Dutch process cocoa
  powder

1 teaspoon instant coffee granules
  (optional)

2 large eggs

1 cup granulated sugar

2 tablespoons packed light
  brown sugar

1 cup cake flour

¼ teaspoon salt

TOPPING

½ cup mini marshmallows

½ cup coarsely chopped pecans

½ cup semisweet chocolate chips

½ cup unsweetened shredded coconut

¼ cup mini peanut butter–chocolate
  cups, chopped (optional)

Preheat the oven to 350°F. Line an 8-inch square pan with parchment paper, and set aside.

In the top of a double boiler, melt the butter and chocolate. Remove from the heat, stir in the cocoa powder and coffee granules (if using), and set aside to cool for 10 minutes.

recipe continues

In the bowl of a stand mixer fitted with the paddle attachment, beat the eggs. Gradually add the granulated and brown sugars. When they are incorporated, add the butter-chocolate mixture and mix to combine. Add the flour and salt and mix just until combined. Scrape the batter into the prepared pan.

Make the topping: In a medium bowl, toss the marshmallows, pecans, chocolate chips, coconut, and peanut butter–chocolate cups (if using), and sprinkle on top of the batter.

Bake until the marshmallows and coconut just start to brown, about 25 minutes. Cool completely in the pan, then cover with plastic wrap and refrigerate for 30 minutes. Remove the cake from the refrigerator and, while it is still chilled, remove the cake from the pan, discard the parchment paper, and cut it in half. Cut each half into 6 thin bars and serve immediately.

VARIATION: ICE-CREAM CAKE

1 Everything Cake, made without the topping, recipe previous page and above

1 pint good-quality ice cream, any flavor

Make the Everything Cake, omitting the topping. While the cake is cooling in the pan, soften the ice cream.

Remove the cooled cake from the pan and discard the parchment. Line the inside of the pan with a piece of plastic wrap that overhangs the sides of the pan a bit.

Cut the cake in half and place one half in the pan. Scrape the softened ice cream onto the half-cake and smooth the top with an offset spatula. Place the other half of the cake on top. Freeze, uncovered, for 20 minutes. Remove the cake from the pan and cut the cake into squares.

recipe continues

VARIATION: LUNCHBOX CAKE

1 Everything Cake, made without the topping, recipe pages 132 and 135
Chocolate Frosting, recipe follows

3 ounces white chocolate, chopped
White quins (candy sequins), for sprinkling

Make the Everything Cake, omitting the topping. Cool in the pan. Remove the cake from the pan and discard the parchment paper.

Make the Chocolate Frosting and smooth on the top of the cake.

In the top of a double boiler, melt the white chocolate. With a spoon, drizzle the white chocolate over the frosted cake and gently swirl with a butter knife. Sprinkle quins on top and refrigerate the cake for 20 minutes to set before cutting into squares.

CHOCOLATE FROSTING

4 ounces bittersweet or semisweet chocolate, chopped

⅓ cup heavy cream

Place the chocolate in a heatproof bowl. In a small saucepan, heat the cream until bubbles begin to appear around the edge (don't boil), and pour over the chocolate in the bowl. Let the mixture sit for 5 minutes, then mix until completely combined. Let the frosting cool completely.

APRICOT RIGHT-SIDE-UP CAKE

An upside-down cake is traditionally made with rings of pineapple, each centered with a cherry to resemble a petaled flower head and placed in the bottom of the pan. After baking, when you flip the cake upside down, the flowers end up on top, soaked with a buttery brown sugar mixture. This dessert is a prettier version—a simple treat to share with someone sweet. · MAKES ONE 4 BY 13-INCH CAKE (SERVES 6)

8 tablespoons unsalted butter,
   plus more for the pan
3 to 4 fresh apricots or
   6 to 8 canned apricot halves
¾ cup granulated sugar,
   plus more for sprinkling

2 large eggs
Finely grated zest of ½ orange
1 teaspoon pure vanilla bean paste
1 cup cake flour
Orange blossom honey,
   for drizzling

Preheat the oven to 350°F. Butter a 4 by 13-inch rectangular tart pan with a removable bottom and set aside.

If using fresh apricots, cut a small X in two places on the skin of each and drop them into boiling water for 1 minute. Peel the skin, halve and discard the pits. If using canned apricots, drain them. Set the apricots aside.

In the bowl of a stand mixer fitted with the paddle attachment, cream the remaining 8 tablespoons butter and the ¾ cup granulated sugar. Add the eggs, then the zest and vanilla bean paste and mix until incorporated. Add the flour and mix just until combined. Scrape into the prepared pan. Place the apricot halves, cut sides down, on top of the batter, making sure that each half does not touch the edges of the pan or another half. Sprinkle some granulated sugar on top of each apricot and bake until set, about 25 minutes.

Cool the cake in the pan for 10 minutes, then remove the sides of the hot pan. Cool the cake completely on the bottom of the pan set on a wire rack.

Cover the cake with plastic wrap and chill in the refrigerator. When ready to serve, remove the cake from the bottom of the pan, cut into wedges, and drizzle with honey.

CHOCOLATE-HAZELNUT-TOPPED CAKE

This simple, spongy cake is made in a tart pan and marbled with an Italian favorite, gianduia—chocolate-hazelnut spread. · MAKES ONE 4 BY 13-INCH CAKE (SERVES 6)

8 tablespoons unsalted butter, softened, plus more for the pan
¾ cup granulated sugar
2 large eggs
1 teaspoon pure vanilla bean paste

1 cup cake flour
¼ cup chocolate-hazelnut spread (gianduia), store-bought, for topping

Preheat the oven to 350°F. Butter a 4 by 13-inch rectangular tart pan with a removable bottom and set aside.

In the bowl of a stand mixer fitted with the paddle attachment, cream the remaining 8 tablespoons butter and the granulated sugar. Beat in the eggs, then the vanilla bean paste. When the vanilla bean paste is incorporated, add the flour and mix just until combined. Scrape into the prepared pan.

Bake until set, about 25 minutes. Cool in the pan for 10 minutes, then remove the sides of the pan (be careful, it will still be very hot). Cool the cake completely on the bottom of the pan set on a wire rack. Cover the cooled cake with plastic wrap and chill in the refrigerator before piping the top.

Pipe the chocolate-hazelnut spread in lines across the width of the cake, and drag a toothpick or knife the length of the cake, alternating directions to make a chevron pattern. Remove the bottom of the pan before cutting the cake.

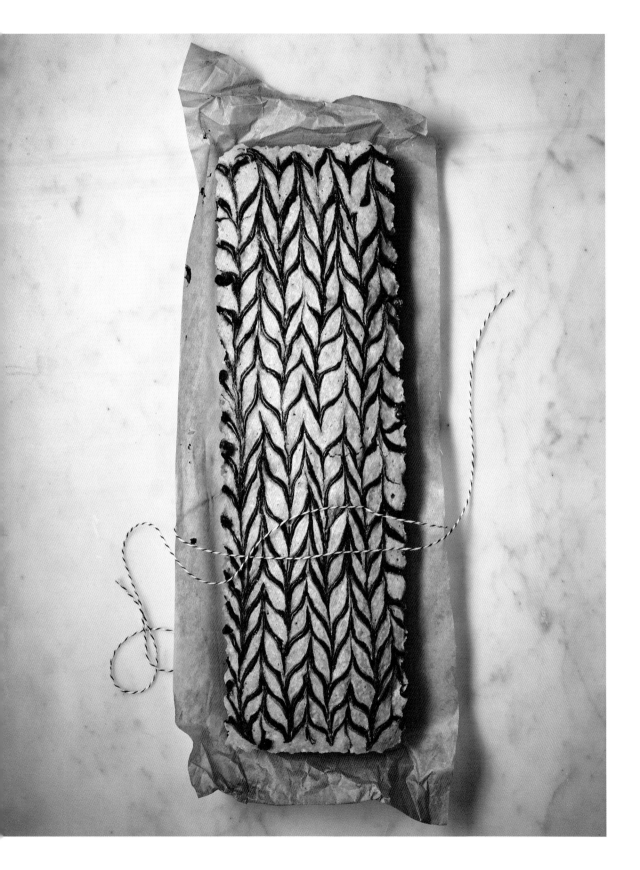

FLOURLESS CHOCOLATE RUM CAKE

Cakes and other desserts were a rare treat in my childhood home. However, we did drive the eight miles into the North End of Boston twice a year to stock up at the Italian bakeries for our holiday open houses, where we served cake and drinks. I remember the young girls behind the bakery counter wrapping our goodies in pink boxes and how they tied them with red and white string and then broke off the ends of the string with their bare hands—very impressive. I also remember the warmth and the aromas of caramelized sugar, yeast, and vanilla, and the holiday music playing in all the shops. We filled the car's trunk with boxes of cookies, ricotta pies, cakes soaked with rum, and a torta della nonna for my grandfather's best friend, Grace. I created this little gem, with a hint of rum flavor, as a small piece of chocolate heaven from my memories of those days. • MAKES ONE 6-INCH ROUND CAKE (SERVES 4 TO 6)

3 tablespoons unsalted butter, softened, plus more for the pan

3 ounces bittersweet or semisweet chocolate, chopped

3 large egg whites

⅛ teaspoon cream of tartar

¼ cup plus 1 tablespoon granulated sugar, divided

2 large egg yolks

½ teaspoon rum

Pinch of salt

Dutch process cocoa powder, for dusting

Preheat the oven to 350°F. Butter the sides of a 6-inch springform pan and line the bottom of the pan with a round of parchment paper. If your pan leaks, line the outside bottom and sides with a piece of aluminum foil.

In the top of a double boiler, melt the remaining 3 tablespoons butter and the chocolate. Remove the top from the heat, stir, and let cool for 15 minutes.

In the bowl of a stand mixer fitted with the whisk attachment, whip the egg whites and cream of tartar. Gradually add ¼ cup of the granulated sugar and

recipe continues

whisk until stiff peaks form. Transfer this mixture to a medium bowl and clean the mixer bowl.

In the clean bowl of your stand mixer fitted with the paddle attachment, beat the egg yolks. Gradually add the remaining 1 tablespoon granulated sugar and beat until thickened. Add the rum, salt, and butter-chocolate mixture and beat to incorporate. With a silicone spatula, gently fold the egg whites into this mixture just until combined. Scrape into the prepared pan and bake until set, about 30 minutes.

Unbuckle and remove the sides of the pan (be careful, it will be very hot), and cool the cake completely on the bottom of the pan set on a wire rack. The cake will cave in as it cools. Remove the cake from the bottom of the pan, remove the parchment round, and dust with cocoa powder just before serving.

PARFAITS

A popular dessert from my childhood is made with chocolate icebox cookies and whipped cream. You spoon some of the cream on a cookie, place another cookie on top, spoon some more whipped cream on top of that, and so on. When you have a tower of these, you gently flip it sideways onto a platter, then smother with lots more whipped cream. Place the platter in the freezer for a bit, and you have a decadent dessert—not exactly a cake. This elegant parfait recipe is based on that all-time favorite. In addition to berries, you can make this with any soft fruit, such as sliced bananas; peeled, pitted, and sliced peaches; or melon balls. Add a layer of granola, and substitute flavored yogurt for the whipped cream, and breakfast is served. • MAKES TWO SMALL PARFAITS (SERVES 2)

2 tablespoons unsalted butter,
   plus more for the pan
¼ cup plus 1 tablespoon
   granulated sugar, divided
1 tablespoon packed light brown sugar
1 large egg
1 large egg yolk
½ teaspoon pure vanilla extract
½ teaspoon orange liqueur

½ cup all-purpose flour
Pinch of salt
Whipped Cream with Orange
   Liqueur, recipe follows
Blueberries, for finishing
Mandarin orange slices, for finishing
Strawberries, for finishing
Raspberries, for finishing
Mint leaves, for finishing

Preheat the oven to 350°F. Butter a 4-inch square pan and set aside.

In the bowl of a stand mixer fitted with the paddle attachment, cream the remaining 2 tablespoons butter, ¼ cup of the granulated sugar, and the brown sugar. Incorporate the egg and egg yolk, then the vanilla and liqueur. Add the flour and salt and mix just until combined. Scrape into the prepared pan and sprinkle the top with the remaining 1 tablespoon granulated sugar. Bake until set, about 15 minutes. Cool completely in the pan.

recipe continues

Using a round cookie cutter slightly smaller in diameter than your serving glasses, cut two rounds of cake. Discard (or eat) the cake scraps, or use them to make an extra parfait. Place some whipped cream on the bottom of each glass, then one cake round on the whipped cream. Top with a layer of blueberries, orange slices, strawberries, and raspberries. Pipe or spoon additional whipped cream on top. Hull any remaining strawberries and cut them in half from the top down. Place these strawberries around the inside of the glass, cut sides out. Pipe more whipped cream inside the circle of strawberries. Top each with one more blueberry and a few mint leaves.

WHIPPED CREAM WITH ORANGE LIQUEUR

½ cup heavy cream	½ teaspoon orange liqueur
1 tablespoon granulated sugar	⅛ teaspoon cream of tartar
½ teaspoon pure vanilla extract	Pinch of salt

In the bowl of a stand mixer fitted with the whisk attachment, start whipping the cream while slowly adding the granulated sugar. Add the vanilla, liqueur, cream of tartar, and salt, and whip until stiff peaks form.

EVERY-DAY CHOCOLATE CAKE

Any day is improved by a little slice of this rich, chocolaty cake and a good cup of tea or coffee. I once made dozens of the chocolate-orange variation of this cake, wrapped in parchment paper and secured with ribbon, for a school bake sale. A teacher told me that she was heartbroken to see the last one sell just before she made it to the table. I baked many more for the teachers' lounge the very next day. Cake makes people happy. · MAKES ONE 6-INCH LOAF CAKE (SERVES 4)

8 tablespoons unsalted butter,
 plus more for the pan
½ cup granulated sugar, plus
 more for the pan
1 ounce bittersweet or semisweet
 chocolate, chopped
½ cup Dutch process cocoa powder,
 plus more for dusting

2 large eggs
¾ teaspoon pure vanilla extract
Grated zest of 1 orange (optional)
½ cup cake flour
¼ teaspoon baking powder
Pinch of salt
Confectioners' sugar, for dusting

Preheat the oven to 350°F. Butter a 6-inch baby loaf pan. Sprinkle some granulated sugar into the pan, shake to coat, discard the excess, and set aside.

In the top of a double boiler, melt the remaining 8 tablespoons butter and the chocolate. Remove from the heat, stir in the cocoa powder, and set aside.

In the bowl of a stand mixer fitted with the paddle attachment, mix the remaining ½ cup granulated sugar, the eggs, vanilla, and orange zest (if using). Incorporate the butter-chocolate mixture. Add the flour, baking powder, and salt and mix just until combined.

Scrape into the prepared pan and bake until set, about 50 minutes. Remove the cake from the hot pan and cool completely on a wire rack. Dust half of the cake with confectioners' sugar and the other half with cocoa powder.

BERRY AND FIG MUFFINS

I love these little cakes. They're easy to whip up, and delicious for a summer picnic. Many muffin recipes call for the butter to be melted. I prefer it creamed. You can use any combination of fresh blueberries, blackberries, strawberries, and raspberries along with the stemmed and halved fresh figs. Another delicious variation is to add a ripe peach or nectarine, peeled, pitted, and chopped into ½-inch cubes. • MAKES FOUR MUFFINS (SERVES 2)

¼ cup granulated sugar,
   plus more for sprinkling
2 tablespoons unsalted butter,
   softened
1 large egg yolk
Finely grated zest of ½ orange
2 tablespoons milk or heavy cream
¾ teaspoon pure vanilla extract

½ cup all-purpose flour
½ teaspoon baking powder
Pinch of salt
½ cup mixed fresh berries
   (such as blueberries, blackberries,
   strawberries, and raspberries) and
   stemmed and halved figs

Preheat the oven to 350°F. Place cupcake papers in four wells of a cupcake pan, and set aside.

In the bowl of a stand mixer fitted with the paddle attachment, cream ¼ cup granulated sugar and the butter. Add the egg yolk and beat until incorporated, then beat in the zest, milk, and vanilla. Add the flour, baking powder, and salt and mix just until combined. With a silicone spatula, fold in the berries and figs.

With a #24 (2.7-tablespoon) spring-loaded scoop, fill the cupcake papers. Sprinkle some granulated sugar on top of the muffins and bake until they start to brown on the edges and are set, about 25 minutes. Cool completely in the pan before removing the muffins from the pan.

ACKNOWLEDGMENTS

I wrote this book, alone in the kitchen with a mountain of recipes, baking hundreds of little cakes for a year. Yet I wasn't by myself. I had the encouragement and generosity of all the bakers, chefs, restaurateurs, teachers, and friends who worked with me in the past. I felt them looking over my shoulder every day.

Thanks to Sandy Gilbert Freidus, editor extraordinaire; publisher Charles Miers; photographer Ellen Silverman, whose light-kissed images are so lovely; amazing designer Jan Derevjanik; baker and stylist Jenny Kellerhals, who made and decorated the pretty cakes; chef Mike Keogh, who was happy to shop for ingredients in the middle of the night; photography assistant Gigi De La Torre; publicist Jessica Napp; copy-editor Natalie Danford; proofreader Tricia Levi; indexer Marilyn Flaig; and production manager Barbara Sadick. I am very lucky to have had their help and support.

To my friends and family, bakers and troublemakers all, who let me have time in the kitchen, and who ate all the cakes: my pastry chef mentor Alina Martell; confidante and chef Cara Tannenbaum; my favorite baker, Nick Malgieri, and Connie Heatter (thank you, Nick and Connie, for Maida's beautiful earrings); Hogan-Murphys, Martinis, Melusos, Randazzo-Gelfmans, Egenbergs, Shapiros, Barer-Whiteheads (CW, who may or may not have based two characters who bake on me), Cohen-Halperins, Rubins, and Pendergasts; Sandy Kellerhals; Anne; Ruta; Christine Burgin and Lola Wegman, Atlas, Bill, the dogs, and Dom; Tanya Bastianich Manuali; Rome; Amy Guittard and chefs Donald Wressell and Josh Johnson, who talked me out of my lifelong fear of white chocolate; and Marc Freidus. To my baking buddies at the beach, Diane, Julia, Lea, Pat, Alysia, and Liv, and the friends who have come to our porch to watch the sunset and eat cake with us every summer weekend for nigh on forty years. And to chef Mark Strausman, who shares lunch with my husband at his restaurant, Mark's Off Madison, all the time. Love you, the FDNY, SVFC, the Red Sox, Zabar's, cousins Jay and Jill, and my Blumenreich, Zabar, and Grimsley families.

To my sweet husband, David, who cooks and baby-wrangles, has let me drag him all over Europe in search of the perfect gold horse charm, and spent an entire day visiting nineteen wholesale bread-baking establishments in Brooklyn so I could find the ultimate olive bread. He makes me, and the Upper West Side, happy. Kisses to the children: Ben, Marki, Danny, Michael, Willie, and little Mary Rose. And my funny valentine and grandson, Brody—this one is for you.

INDEX

USEFUL SOURCE

ZABAR'S
AND COMPANY

2245 Broadway
New York, New York
10024
(800) 697-6301
www.zabars.com

The ultimate source for kitchen equipment and baking ingredients.

U.S. AND METRIC CONVERSION CHARTS

All conversions are approximate.

WEIGHT CONVERSIONS

U.S.	METRIC
½ ounce	14 g
1 ounce	28 g
1½ ounces	43 g
2 ounces	57 g
2½ ounces	71 g
3 ounces	85 g
3½ ounces	100 g
4 ounces	113 g
5 ounces	142 g
6 ounces	170 g
7 ounces	200 g
8 ounces	227 g
9 ounces	255 g
10 ounces	284 g
11 ounces	312 g
12 ounces	340 g
13 ounces	368 g
14 ounces	400 g
15 ounces	425 g
1 pound	454 g

OVEN TEMPERATURES

°F	GAS MARK	°C
250	½	120
275	1	140
300	2	150
325	3	165
350	4	180
375	5	190
400	6	200
425	7	220
450	8	230
475	9	240
500	10	260
550	Broil	290

LIQUID CONVERSIONS

U.S.	METRIC
1 teaspoon	5 ml
1 tablespoon	15 ml
2 tablespoons	30 ml
3 tablespoons	45 ml
¼ cup	60 ml
⅓ cup	75 ml
⅓ cup plus 1 tablespoon	90 ml
⅓ cup plus 2 tablespoons	100 ml
½ cup	120 ml
⅔ cup	150 ml
¾ cup	180 ml
¾ cup plus 2 tablespoons	200 ml
1 cup	240 ml
1 cup plus 2 tablespoons	275 ml
1¼ cups	300 ml
1⅓ cups	325 ml
1½ cups	350 ml
1⅔ cups	375 ml
1¾ cups	400 ml
1¾ cups plus 2 tablespoons	450 ml
2 cups (1 pint)	475 ml
2½ cups	600 ml
3 cups	725 ml
4 cups (1 quart)	945 ml
(1,000 ml = 1 liter)	

First Published in the
United States of America in 2023 by
Rizzoli International Publications, Inc.
300 Park Avenue South
New York, NY 10010
www.rizzoliusa.com

©2023 Tracey Zabar
Photography by Ellen Silverman

Publisher: Charles Miers
Editor: Sandra Gilbert Freidus
Design: Jan Derevjanik
Design Assistance: Olivia Russin
Baker: Jenny Kellerhals
Production Manager: Barbara Sadick
Copy-editor: Natalie Danford
Proofreader: Tricia Levi
Indexer: Marilyn Flaig
Managing Editor: Lynn Scrabis

Printed in China

2023 2024 2025 2026/10 9 8 7 6 5 4 3 2 1
ISBN: 978-0-8478-7362-3
Library of Congress Control Number:
2023933592

Visit us online:
Facebook.com/RizzoliNewYork
instagram.com/rizzolibooks
twitter.com/Rizzoli_Books
pinterest.com/rizzolibooks
youtube.com/user/RizzoliNY
issuu.com/Rizzoli

Visit Tracey Zabar online: traceyzabar.com

A portion of the proceeds from each book benefits
Engine Company 74 of the New York City Fire
Department (FDNY) and the Saltaire Volunteer
Fire Company (SVFC).